OCR ⇒

Chicago Public Library

REFERENCE

Form 178 rev. 1-94

SERVE IT FORTH

COOKING WITH
ANNE McCAFFREY

SERVE IT FORTH

→FORTH←

COOKING WITH
ANNE McCAFFREY

EDITED BY
ANNE McCAFFREY WITH
JOHN GREGORY BETANCOURT

ASPECT®

WARNER BOOKS

A Time Warner Company

Aspect name and logo are registered trademarks of Warner Books, Inc.

Warner Books, Inc., 1271 Avenue of the Americas, New York, NY 10020
Visit our Web site at
http://pathfinder.com/twep

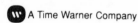 A Time Warner Company

Printed in the United States of America

First Printing: October 1996

10 9 8 7 6 5 4 3 2 1

Library of Congress Cataloging-in-Publication Data
Serve it forth : cooking with Anne McCaffrey / edited by Anne
  McCaffrey with John Betancourt.
        p. cm.
  ISBN 0-446-67161-4
  1. Cookery. I. McCaffrey, Anne. II. Betancourt, John.
TX714.S47 1996
641.5—dc20   96-20293
                                                                     CIP

Cover design by Pat Morrissey
Book design by John Betancourt

ATTENTION: SCHOOLS AND CORPORATIONS
WARNER books are available at quantity discounts with bulk purchase for educational, business, or sales promotional use. For information, please write to: SPECIAL SALES DEPARTMENT, WARNER BOOKS, 1271 AVENUE OF THE AMERICAS, NEW YORK, N.Y. 10020

For Virginia Kidd

The authors of this book have kindly agreed
to donate their profits to the
Science Fiction and Fantasy Writers of America's
Emergency Medical Fund.

Contents

Serve It Forth!

When all of us science fiction writers were once unpublished—which, surprising as it may seem, once we were—we were often forced to cook for ourselves and cook the viands we could afford. Those of us who could Read The Manual resorted to cookbooks or gratefully remembered grandmaternal recipes that could be produced cheaply: "cheap" being very much the first operative word. And "fast" being the second one. You made a meal—when you couldn't abide the hunger pangs any longer because it interrupted your writing—preferably a quick, as well as cheap meal, and often something that could be reheated later and still not taste too bad. (Of course, with the advent of microwave ovens and the plethora of inexpensive fast food eateries in most localities, "quick" and "reheat" are no longer pejorative. However, not all of us live where it's easy to get to fast fooderies.) My son, Todd, used to whomp up a pot of something or other in quantities that would suffice him all week.

Oddly enough, he often used recipes from *Cooking Out of This World*. (Nice child, he is.) So perhaps *Serve It Forth* will be helpful as well as collectible.

In the McCaffrey household, when we had transferred to Ireland, we survived what the family called "the pancake years." Quoth my daughter often in a piteous tone, "Wouldn't it be nice to have pancakes only when we *wanted* them?" I remember a time when the financial situation was no longer so dire, when Gigi, Alec, and I went to a Creperie in Boston because we really "wanted pancakes" and burst into laughter when we realized what we were doing. There is, I might add, no recipe for pancakes in this volume. Nor in *Cooking Out of This World*.

Speaking of which, I should put the record straight on how it came to be in the first place: T'was Betty Ballantine who had the felicitous inspiration for the first s-f writers' cookbook. She offered me the contract to produce the volume as much because she knew I could cook cheap, fast and well as because she knew I needed every cent I could get my hands on after my divorce and move to Ireland. It is the one book of the 55 I have since published that never made back its advance: as much because 1) I wasn't well known then and 2) the booksellers, God love 'em, didn't know where to put it—in with cookbooks or with s-f.[1] Copies now fetch as much as $400.00 when one can be found in good condition. Who'd've thunk it?

Let me also remind readers that it was Virginia Kidd who put *Cooking Out of This World* together since I was in Ireland. We didn't want the post to lose valuable recipes. T'was she who suggested that we keep the accompanying letters because some of them were more priceless than the recipes.

I always smile at Avram Davidson's "put water in a pot apartly." How could we *not* print that?

I am also amused to discover how many of us have learned to cook since 1970: Peter Beagle, for instance. And those of us who have improved.

And there are lots of the new kids on the block represented now who will be as collectible later on, I hope, as I was.

Thanks to John Betancourt who has reprinted the original deathless, priceless *Cooking Out of This World*, and to Betsy Mitchell who thought it would be neat to do another s-f writers' cookbook since there are so many more of us these days. Maybe, <grin>, by eating goods which have sustained those of us who created new worlds and fantasies, dear reader will ingest the magic that goes into making science fiction so much fun for us to write.

So browse through, pick the food of your choice, cook it, and gladly *Serve It Forth!*

—Anne McCaffrey
Dragonhold-Underhill, Ireland

---

[1]Note to booksellers: please place this volume in both categories: Science Fiction *and* Cookery.

SERVE IT FORTH

COOKING WITH
ANNE McCAFFREY

David M. Alexander is an attorney-at-law who also finds time to write novels, including The Chocolate Spy *(1978),* Fane *(1981), and* My Real Name is Lisa *(1996). He also writes articles about computer programming for computer magazines—a multitalented man.*

David M. Alexander

₩D

Creamy Pasta Sauce

I created this recipe because I was tired of standard red pasta sauces. I find it difficult to find a red sauce with a strong yet not-bitter or acidic flavor. I knew I wanted to start with a garlic and butter sauce, and the rest of the ingredients were mostly trial and error. While this sauce is more complicated than a standard Alfredo sauce, I think it is also much tastier. It is definitely neither low calorie nor low fat, but if the pasta is served together with salad, vegetables, bread, and a light meat such as boneless chicken breast or lean pork loin, the amount of sauce contained in a normal serving of the pasta will be relatively small, probably only a few tablespoons.

Ingredients

1 stick of butter
½ sweet red or yellow onion
4 to 6 cherry tomatoes (or 3 roma tomatoes)
to taste: black pepper, onion powder, garlic granules, parsley flakes, cilantro
    flakes, chives, red pepper flakes, tobasco
2 pinches of sugar (tomato seeds are bitter)
1 or 2 (or 3 or 4) pinches of herbes de Provance
¼ cup heavy cream
white wine (optional)

Directions

Quantity of pasta for 1 to 2.
Melt butter in saucepan.
Cut ½ sweet red or yellow onion and chop into small pieces.
Sauté onion in butter under low to moderate heat until it is very soft and translucent.

Chop 4 to 6 cherry tomatoes or 3 roma tomatoes (or up to 1 fresh tomato) into relatively small pieces. You can also add a few pieces of sun-dried tomato if you like.

Add tomato pieces to butter, sauté.

Add black pepper, onion powder, garlic granules, parsley flakes, cilantro flakes, chives, and 2 pinches of sugar (tomato seeds are bitter), and 1 or 2 (or 3 or 4) pinches of herbes de Provence. I like to add a pinch of red pepper flakes. Make sure you use lots of garlic. You can use fresh parsely and fresh chives, but add them at the end so that they retain their flavor.

Optionally, add a splash or two of white wine.

When tomatoes are *very* soft, add ¼ cup heavy cream. Mix until the mixture is creamy and slightly pink. If you like, add a couple of dashes of tabasco. Correct seasoning to taste; usually salt is not needed.

Serve on pasta with grated asiago cheese.

Note: Cream and butter will normally separate unless you do this step: whip mixture while hot with a wire whip. Then, mix in a small quantity of a mixture of water and corn starch—slowly—until the sauce begins to thicken. The thickened sauce will not separate. Make sure that it is thick enough to coat the back of a spoon. Be careful not to add too much or too little of the cornstarch mixture.

Lori Allen teaches part time freshman English at the University of Bridgeport. Her science fiction and fantasy stories have appeared in quite a few magazines, most notably The Magazine of Fantasy & Science Fiction, Rod Serling's The Twilight Zone Magazine, The Horror Show, *and* Tomorrow. *Currently she lives in Connecticut with her husband, poet Dick Allen.*

Lori Negridge Allen

🍴

Marvelous Morphed Meat

My mother never taught me to cook, thank heavens.

Which is not to imply Mom was a bad cook. Quite the contrary. Her specialties approached haut cuisine; next to her borscht, all other borschts are merely beet soups. The problem is, in order to make that borscht she had to first make the cabasa, even though there is no cabasa in borscht.

Cabasa, for those who are Slavonically deprived, is a sausage—either boiled (the way my mother made it) or smoked (the way it's generally sold in stores). To make cabasa, Mom first boiled pig intestines, then she disgustingly filled them with coarsely chopped pork and spices, then she boiled them until the pork lost all its pinkness, and half an hour longer to be safe, then, some two hours down the line, she put aside the cabasa and started to make the borscht from the water in which the cabasa had been cooked.

I do not know, nor do I want to know how she would have complicated up this utterly simple, in fact nearly foolproof (the only thing you can do wrong is undercook it, and that's one of the reasons microwaves were invented) recipe.

It was my first marital cooking foray beyond the standard meat and potatoes. In that incarnation, it was made on top of the stove, with whatever ingredients came to hand. It vaguely resembled my mother's stuffed cabbage, but I couldn't call it "stuffed cabbage" because there wasn't any stuffing to do or any cabbage in it, so I named it "chopped meat mess." Or tried to.

My husband, the poet, rebelled. But the dish itself made him spout sonnets and odes. It reminded him of something his mother (a direct descendent from the *Mayflower* who couldn't tell the difference between a blintz and a pyroghi) used to make. She called it "Russian Baked Meat"—until Korea, when Russian meant Communist and Communist meant the enemy and my Yankee mother-in-law fought the Cold War on the Home Front by renaming it "MacArthur Baked Meat."

General MacArthur by now having truly faded away, I tried to reyclept it "Morphed Meat." But the poet again rebelled. Because "Morphed Meat" didn't sound very tasty. And because of insufficient alliteration. "Call it 'Marvelous Morphed Meat,'" he offered. And so I shall.

Ingredients (amounts of all ingredients are approximate)

    1 cup cooked rice
    1 pound diet lean chopped meat
    ¼ cup chopped onions
    ¼ cup chopped green pepper
    1 cup spaghetti sauce or stewed tomatoes
    choice of any or all to taste—salt, pepper, garlic powder, oregano, basil,
        chili powder

Directions

    To make it, mix cooked rice, chopped meat, onions, chopped green pepper, spaghetti sauce or stewed tomatoes, plus your choice of any or all to taste—salt, pepper, garlic powder, oregano, basil, chili powder. Spoon into greased casserole. Bake (uncovered if you like it the dry MacArthur way, covered if you like it the stuffed cabbage-without-the-cabbage way) at 350 degrees for about 90 minutes. (If short of time, increase oven heat and stir two or three times during cooking.) Serve with extra tomato sauce and shredded cheddar or Parmesan cheese. Goes especially good with corn. Serves 4.

Poul Anderson was born in Pennsylvania of Scandinavian parents—hence the spelling of the first name—and raised mostly in Texas and later on a farm in Minnesota. He majored in physics at the University of Minnesota but soon went into writing as a career. He and his wife and occasional collaborator Karen have lived for many years near San Francisco, except when traveling. Among his best-known works, some of which have won awards, are Brain Wave, The High Crusade, Tau Zero, The Broken Sword, Operation Chaos, The Time Patrol, The Boat of a Million Years, *and* Harvest of Stars.

These recipes yield tasty food if the ingredients are good and fresh—a sine qua non of any proper cooking, after all—and have the additional virtue of being easy. Some are Poul's own invention; others are due to friends and included with their permission.

Poul Anderson

🍴

Cucumber Karina

This recipe is, of course, by my wife, Karen.

Directions

Peel, quarter, seed, and slice a cucumber. Shake in a plastic bag with 1 tablespoon of seasoned wok oil and ½ teaspoon sesame seeds. Microwave on high for 5 minutes.

🍴

She has also devised what we both call:

The Great Pumpkin

Directions

Take 1 of the mini-pumpkins that will fit in a baking dish, cut the top off level so it can be put back, scoop out seeds and fiber. Take 1 or 2 filets of pork and cut across to make thick chunks. Put half this meat in the pumpkin. Add dry onion, dry mushroom, juniper berries, salt, pepper, and Accent to taste. Pour in boiling water or stock to cover. Put in the rest of the meat. Cap the pumpkin, place it in the baking dish, and bake in a preheated 400 degree oven for 30 minutes. Reduce heat to 350 degrees for another 30 to 60 minutes depending on size.

To serve, empty out the contents, cut the pumpkin meat away from the rind, and mingle it with the rest.

¶⫯

Parsley Kraken

Directions

Sauté chopped garlic and onion in generous amount of olive oil. Add squid or squid parts—fresh is far preferable to frozen—and water or white wine, about 2 teaspoons of lemon juice, and a dash of the strong Oriental fish sauce known as Nuoc Mam. Simmer. In serving, thick slices of French bread are recommended to sop up the juice.

¶⫯

Whitefish Béla

This one I came up with in days when we were active in The Society for Creative Anachronism, I under the name of Sir Béla of Eastmarch. The knighthood wasn't self-bestowed, it was awarded for prowess in sword-and-shield combat. We were all younger once.

Directions

In olive oil sauté plenty of minced garlic—1 large clove or 2 small— together with a chopped bay leaf and rosemary. Add white wine and a few dashes of Angostura bitters (or dry vermouth alone) and heat a little more. Lay in your filet(s) of halibut, turbot, or other whitefish and season with turmeric and pepper. Poach about 5 minutes, turning it over at midpoint, and cover with slivered almonds.

My quondam collaborator Mildred Downey Broxon once created a dish she roguishly dubbed Cod Piece. It was superb, but elaborate, and for my own use I simplified it to:

🍴

Oh My Cod

Directions

Sauté chopped green onions. Add vegetable stock or V-8, lemon juice to taste, chopped garlic, a bit of tarragon and rosemary, small dashes of soy and Worcestershire sauce. Simmer down to about half the volume. Put in cod and poach. The sauce goes well onto bread, rice, or potatoes.

Making things up as I went along, one evening when there wasn't much in the house, I think I did pretty well with:

🍴

Tuna Improvisa

Directions

Put olive oil in pan. Add 1 or more small cans of water-packed tuna and heat gently, with generous amounts of lemon juice and Japanese seasoning (e.g., prepared seaweed or beefsteak plant). Add sliced scallions and mushrooms (preferably Crimini) and cook a little longer. Serve over baguettes, with a green salad or the like.

My brother John is a really good cook. He has passed on to me:

🍴

Lemon-Curry Chicken in Pita Bread

Ingredients

1 roasted chicken breast half
1/3 cup plain yogurt
1 tablespoon chutney
1 tablespoon lemon juice
3/4 tablespoon curry powder

2 tablespoons minced carrot
2 tablespoons minced bell pepper or celery or both
pinch salt
shredded lettuce
2 pita breads

Directions

Finely dice the chicken and combine with all the other ingredients except lettuce and pita bread. Cut heated pita bread in halves, stuff pockets with chicken mixture, and top with shredded lettuce.

For weight watchers, our friend Heather MacKenzie has devised what I call:

ᵀⅅ

Potatoes MacKenzie

Directions

Cut up potatoes and spray with nonstick spray. Shake in a plastic bag with bread crumbs and nonfat Parmesan cheese (about equal amounts of both), garlic powder, onion powder, and chili powder (to taste, but not stingy). Spread on sprayed cookie sheet and bake 30 to 45 minutes at 350 degrees, or until done and a bit brown.

When I do this, instead of the spray I stir the potatoes around in a bowl with about 1 tablespoon of olive oil, and use regular Parmesan. Different seasonings can be substituted, too.

Finally, by way of dessert, here's another recipe by Karen. We put it on our Christmas cards one year, and it was a great success among the people who tried it.

ᵀⅅ

Berry Crispness Cookies

Ingredients

1 (15-ounce) can sweetened condensed milk
1½ cups rolled oats, regular or quick-cooking

½ cup coarsely broken walnuts
½ cup sweetened dried cranberries
½ teaspoon ground cinnamon
½ teaspoon salt
nonstick spray
flour

Directions

Heat oven to 325 degrees. Spray two 10 x 14-inch cookie sheets with vegetable spray. Dust with flour and shake off excess.

Combine milk and oats in a medium-size bowl. Stir in nuts, berries, cinnamon, and salt. Drop by teaspoonful onto cookie sheets, flattening gently with back of spoon. Bake 15 minutes, until golden brown. Cool on rack.

Makes 4 dozen small cookies.

Patricia Anthony has taught on the university level in both Portugal and Brazil and has sold everything from cars to real estate. She currently works part time at The Dallas Morning News. *Her first novel,* Cold Allies, *was named one of the three best science fiction books of 1993 by* Publishers Weekly *and won the* Locus Reader's Poll *for Best First Novel. Her other novels include* Brother Termite, Conscience of the Beagle, Happy Policeman, Cradle of Splendor, *and* God's Fires.

Patricia Anthony

🍴

The If-You-Serve-This-They'll-Swear-You're-Hispanic Queso

Ingredients

1 very large or 2 medium onions, minced
5 large cloves of garlic, minced
1 tablespoon cumin seeds
1 large or 2 medium fresh tomatoes, minced
24 ounces Velveeta, cubed (you may use Velveeta Light, if you choose)
1 (8-ounce) package grated cheddar or Montery Jack
a good picante sauce (Mexican hot sauce)
1 fresh jalepeño pepper, very finely chopped (optional)
salt to taste

Directions

Grease the bottom of your slow cooker and turn to high. Sauté onions and garlic until onions are transparent. Add the cumin seeds and the minced fresh tomato. When the tomato is cooked, reduce heat to *medium* and add Velveeta a little at a time, stirring gently as the Velveeta melts. Turn heat to *low*. Add the grated cheddar, alternating that with hot sauce to your taste, and the jalepeño pepper if you want more spice. Serve with tortilla chips.

🍴D

The I've-Been-to-Brazil-I-Know-What-Black-Beans-Are Dip

Ingredients

3 cups dried black beans
3 cans Ro-Tel (If you absolutely *have* to, you may substitute with 3 cans
    stewed tomatoes and 3 to 4 chopped jalepeño peppers)
1 very large onion, minced
1 head (not just clove) garlic, minced
3 tablespoons cumin seeds
3 bay leaves
3 handfuls of fresh cilantro (coriander) leaves (optional)
salt to taste

Directions

Wash beans. Soak overnight in a large bowl with scant water to cover and the 3 cans of Ro-Tel. Dump everything but the cilantro into a large soup pot and cook on low. When beans are tender, add the chopped cilantro and cook another hour. Remove the bay leaves. At this point, you may put the dip in a slow cooker to keep warm and serve with chips, or you may put the mixture through your food processor to puree and then serve.

⚔

The I-Stole-This-Mexican-Chicken-and-Dumpling-Recipe-and-then-Changed-It-So-Much-That-Not-Even-Its-Mama,-an-Intellectual-Property-Lawyer,-Would-Recognize-It Main Dish

Ingredients

6 inside stalks of celery with the leaves, chopped
1 large onion, minced
3 handfuls fresh parsley, chopped
1 handful cilantro (coriander) leaves, chopped (optional)
3 bay leaves
1 tablespoon cumin seeds
3 pounds chicken tenders, minced
1 to 2 large jars Cheez Whiz
2 packages flour tortillas, sliced into strips
salt to taste

Directions

Grease bottom of a large soup pot. Sauté celery, onion, parsley and cilantro until tender. Add 2 quarts of water, bay leaves, cumin seeds, and bring to boil. Add chicken tenders. When chicken tenders are done, reduce heat and remove bay leaves. Add Cheez Whiz slowly, stirring all the while, until mixture thickens. Add strips of flour tortillas, taking care to separate them with a fork. *Turn off the heat immediately.* Serve.

Peter Beagle says he learned a great deal about cooking "from the books—far too few—of Marian Burros, who I think is the food critic for the New York Times these days. Glimpsed her once on TV and promptly stood up and saluted—'Our Leader.' These recipes aren't hers, but I'd never have been able to get them together without her patient printed counsel and advice. Later for Julia Child."

Mr. Beagle is also the author of The Last Unicorn *and a number of other classic novels.*

Peter S. Beagle

🍴

Beagle's Legendary Minestrone

To paraphrase Coleridge badly, we cooketh best what we loveth best. I loveth soup: all kinds, but especially the sort that borders on being a stew but refrains daintily from taking that final irrevocable step. Here are three of my stalwart staples.

Ingredients

2 quarts of water
3 tablespoons of beef stock base or bouillon
3 tablespoons of tomato paste
1 whole onion, diced
salt
garlic
1 cup of carrots
1 cup of lima beans
1 cup of celery
2 tablespoons of fresh parsley
1 teaspoon of Bouquet Garni
1 cup of green beans
1 cup of peas
1 cup of zucchini
½ a cup of spinach or Swiss chard (optional)
1 cup of elbow macaroni
grated Parmesan or Romano cheese (optional)

Directions

To 2 quarts of water, add 3 tablespoons of whatever beef stock base or bouillon you've got handy. Add 3 tablespoons of tomato paste, 1 whole onion, diced, maybe a little salt, and as much garlic as family unity will stand. Bring to a boil and simmer for 10 to 15 minutes. Then add a cup of carrots, a cup of lima beans, a cup of celery, 2 tablespoons of fresh parsley, and a teaspoon of Bouquet Garni. Simmer for another 30 minutes; then add a cup of green beans (fresh, frozen, doesn't matter), a cup of peas (ditto), and a cup of zucchini. Sometimes I toss in half a cup or so of spinach or Swiss chard; sometimes not. When the vegetables are *almost* tender, add a cup of elbow macaroni and continue simmering until everything's done. (Go by the limas—they always seem to take the longest.) Sprinkle with grated Parmesan or Romano cheese if desired. Good stuff. Heals the sick, raises the dead, pacifies the obnoxious.

🍴

Beagle's My-God-You-Mean-They're-Coming-for-*Lunch?* Zucchini Soup

Quick and absolutely foolproof, speaking as a fool.

Ingredients

4 cups of chopped, unpeeled zucchini
1 onion, diced
2 cups of chicken broth
2 tablespoons of margarine
1 to 2 cups of parsley, chopped
¼ teaspoon of nutmeg

Directions

Summer 4 cups of chopped, unpeeled zucchini and a diced onion in 2 cups of chicken broth. When the zucchini is tender, add 2 tablespoons of margarine, 1 to 2 cups of chopped parsley, and ¼ teaspoon of nutmeg (very important). Let the soup cool for a few minutes; then puree it in a blender on low speed. Goes with absolutely everything.

Beagle's Comforting Clam Chowder

For Very Bad Days.

Ingredients

sliced mushrooms
2 washed and diced leeks (or 1 large onion)
butter
garlic
2 cans cream of potato soup
2 cans nonfat or lowfat milk
2 cans of chopped clams
sherry to taste (optional)
salt and/or pepper
bacon

Directions

Sauté a lot of sliced mushrooms and 2 washed and diced leeks or one large diced onion in butter and garlic. Plenty of garlic. Then add 2 cans of cream of potato soup and 2 cans of nonfat or lowfat milk. Stir in 2 cans of chopped clams—adding sherry to taste (optional, but a nice thought), season with salt and/or pepper (a little cayenne is nice), and sprinkle a generous handful of bacon atop. Crank up a suitable old movie—*Captains Courageous* is a bit obvious, but *The Crimson Pirate* goes very well with this dish.

M. Shayne Bell's two novels, Nicoji and Inuit, have been attracting a wide fan following, as have his numerous short stories. He writes medical software documentation for his day job and spends his spare time hiking around the Utah desert, finding the abandoned cities of the Anasazi.

M. Shayne Bell

¶D

The food of Brazil is as colorful as the country itself. Brazilians take the time to present their food beautifully, and they decorate everything—from potato salads to corn puddings—with fruits, vegetables, and cheeses placed over the top in geometric patterns. You hesitate to take the first spoonful and mar the art.

I lived in Brazil for two years. When it came time to leave, I regretted most the foods I thought I would never eat again. I tried to recreate some from memory when I got home, and what follows are the successes. Bon apetite.

Pudim de Milho, do Brasil (Brazilian Corn Pudding)

Ingredients

6 ears of corn (or one regular size package of frozen corn, thawed—if you use this, you'll probably need a little more corn starch)
1 liter of whole milk (roughly 1 quart)
2 cups of sugar
vanilla to taste
3 tablespoons corn starch
cinnamon
coconut
fruit to decorate with
whipped cream

Directions

Cut the corn from the cobs (or thaw the frozen corn). Put the corn and some of the milk in a blender and blend. Strain out the corn pulp. Put the liquid in a pot, add the rest of the milk, sugar, vanilla, and corn starch. Cook over low heat, stirring constantly, until the mixture boils and thickens (it will not get very thick at this point). Pour onto a platter or into a bowl and refrigerate (now it will get thick). When cool, sprinkle with cinnamon and cover with coconut. Decorate in geometric patterns with any kind of fruit, and use as many as possible: bananas, apples, papayas, grapes, pineapple, strawberries, kiwi fruit, cherries, oranges, raspberries, mango slices—the more tropical the fruit, the more authentic. If you use bananas, apples, or pears, put the slices in a bowl, squeeze lime juice on them, and marinate for a few minutes before you put them on the pudding; this keeps them from going brown. After serving, top with whipped cream.

Serves 8 to 10 people.

¶D

Salada de Batata, do Brasil (Brazilian Potato Salad)

Ingredients

10 medium-size potatoes
9 eggs
3 stalks celery
4 large carrots
2 bags frozen peas
1 pound precooked ham
1 yellow onion
1 red onion
1 each of red, green, and yellow peppers
1 quart homemade mayonnaise (or 1 bottle Kraft mayonnaise [not Miracle Whip or salad dressing, which would mask the flavors of all the foods you are combining])
other vegetables, nuts, and meats as desired
fruit, vegetables, and cheese to decorate with

Directions

Cut the potatoes into small pieces and boil them. Hard boil the eggs and chop them into fine pieces. Dice the celery and carrots and cook them. Heat the peas, but do not boil. Dice the ham, onions, and peppers. Mix all of these together, then add the following to taste: salt, oregano, garlic, black pepper. Add mayonnaise and stir (you want the salad moist, not dry;

I find that when you can stir the salad easily, you then have enough mayonnaise). This makes the main salad, but you can also add diced cucumbers and olives, grated cheese of any kind, pineapple, raisins, nuts of all kinds (but especially cashews or walnuts), chicken, shrimp, sausage, and bacon. Pour the salad onto a platter and shape it into a mound. Decorate it with a ring of cherry tomatoes cut in half around the base, with parsley sprigs placed between the tomatoes. Decorate the rest of the salad in geometric patterns with green olives, black olives, grapes, different colors of cheese, kiwi fruit, pineapple, apples, strawberries, cucumbers, cashews, Brazil nuts, avocados, mango and papaya slices. Chill for at least 2 hours.

Serves 10 to 15 people.

One of the late, great John Brunner's last contributions to the field were these recipes, sent in shortly before his death. He is best known for his Hugo Award–winning novel The Sheep Look Up, *among many, many classics of the field.*

John Brunner

🍴

Lamb Sapphire

This has nothing to do with precious stones. I invented it for—and it was much enjoyed by—a pretty young woman from Sri Lanka called Nilmini, whose name turned out to mean sapphire.

Ingredients

1 small onion
1 medium carrot
1 pound/450 gm lamb
1 (14-ounce/400 gm) tin of tomatoes
sea salt, black pepper q.s.
1 teaspoon brown sugar
½ teaspoon dried basil
2 medium-size potatoes

Directions for two

Preheat oven to gas mark 4 or equivalent (180°C, 350°F). In a suitable casserole fry, preferably in homemade dripping with plenty of jelly, a small onion, peeled and sliced. When it starts to brown, add a carrot sliced thin. Stir thoroughly.

Move the vegetables aside and sear 4 to 6 pieces of stewing lamb, total weight about 1 pound/450 gm including bone. When browned on all sides, add a tin of tomatoes, juice included, plus sea salt and black pepper to taste, brown sugar, and dried basil. Crush the tomatoes well and mix all together. Make sure the meat is below the level of the juice. Bring to the boil and simmer for a few moments.

Cover and cook for 1 hour high in the oven. Transfer to lowest shelf, increase heat to gas mark 6 (200°C, 425°F), and bake at the top shelf two medium potatoes, scrubbed, wiped with oil, and sprinkled with a little sea salt, until done (about 40 minutes). Good with a watercress salad.

🍴

Bacon Roly-Poly

I have been told by American friends that this is unknown the other side of the Herring Pond. Amazing. It's delicious. Here's a slightly modernized version of an old British favourite.

Ingredients

4 ounces/120 gm self-raising flour (and more for dusting board)
1½ ounces/50 gm suet
water q.s.
3 large rashers back bacon
1 small onion
1 tablespoon parsley, chopped
sea salt, black pepper q.s.

Directions for two

Using a broad-bladed knife, mix self-raising flour with prepared shredded suet and a little sea salt. Add sufficient water, a splash at a time, to make a sticky dough.

Turn it out on a well-floured board and sprinkle more flour on top. Roll into an oblong a little longer and wider than your bacon. Dust on more flour if the rolling-pin sticks.

Lay lengthways on top three large rashers of back bacon, close together but without overlapping. Slice a small onion thinly and scatter over, plus a generous tablespoonful of chopped parsley and several grinds of black pepper.

Using a palette knife, loosen the dough from the board. If it sticks put a little more flour under. Roll up carefully and press in the ends.

Sprinkle a large enough sheet of aluminum foil with flour. Carefully transfer the roll to the middle of it. Bring the wide sides of the foil together above the roll, pleat and fold down, then fold over the ends to make a neat packet.

Steam, tightly covered, for about 2½ hours; a little longer will do no harm.

Serve with stewed tomatoes, or onion gravy and a green vegetable such as spinach or kale.

Bon appetit!

Lois McMaster Bujold picked up her early interest in science fiction (and in desserts) from her father, an engineering professor at Ohio State University. Her writing efforts began in junior high school, but she did not begin writing for serious professional publication until 1982. She wrote three novels in three years and, in 1985, all three sold to Baen Books.

She has gone on to write a dozen novels for Baen, winning along the way quite a few awards for her tales of Miles Vorkosigan. Her work has been translated into a baker's dozen languages.

Lois McMaster Bujold

🍴

Sherried Walnut Cake

I recall that the flurry of experimentation which resulted in the walnut cake was kicked off by my reading a lady's memoir about her Viennese childhood and Viennese pastries, several years before I began writing my novels—there was more *time* in those days.

Ingredients (have all ingredients at room temperature)

2 cups (about ½ pound) ground walnuts
3 eggs
¾ cup sugar
½ cup cake flour
1 teaspoon baking powder
¼ teaspoon salt
½ cup very soft butter
1 tablespoon sherry
$^2/_3$ cup sherry or marsala wine
$^2/_3$ cup honey
8 to 12 walnut halves

Directions

The walnuts can be chopped in a blender, one cup at a time, on high speed for about 10 seconds.

Beat the eggs and sugar together at high speed in the large bowl of an electric mixer until they are very light and fluffy; this usually takes at least 5 minutes. Sift together the flour, baking powder, and salt.

Gently fold in the nuts, flour mixture, butter, and tablespoon of sherry, alternating about a fourth of each at a time.

Pour the batter into an 8- or 9-inch cake pan lined on the bottom with a heavily buttered circle of wax paper, cut to fit. Bake the cake 40 to 50 minutes at 300 degrees or until a toothpick or knife-blade inserted in the center comes out clean.

While the cake is cooling (about 10 minutes), heat the sherry and honey together in a small saucepan just to a simmer. Invert the cake on a cake plate and gently peel off the wax paper. Drizzle the hot honey and sherry mixture evenly over the cake until it is soaked through. Decorate with a ring of walnut halves.

Chris Bunch, coauthor of the Sten science fiction series and the first three epic fantasy novels of the Anteros, lives on the Washington coast in the world's smallest town with his best friend, Karen. He is currently working on the next two novels of the Shadow Warrior trilogy, as well as a huge fantasy trilogy, the first volume of which is The Seer King.

Chris Bunch

🍴

We (meaning my former partner Allan Cole and myself) put at least two recipes in our *Sten* series. Since Cole was a Cordon Bleú chef, and I like to mess about in the kitchen, all of the recipes were well-tried and worth doing. Perhaps, in the final volume, we got a trifle silly—putting in the recipe for the world's most difficult beef jerky, for instance, or referring to a spineless animal as an *amoebus quaylus*. But I guess you're entitled to get weird when you come to the end of a series.

The first three dishes make a wonderful and complete meal. It's to be noted that the first has a *lot* of garlic in it, not only enough to run any vampires into the next province, but will make Anne Rice break her dinner engagement with you and, if cooked anywhere near Bram Stoker's grave, may be cause for a Major Surprise. It isn't really all that hot, unlike some Thai recipes, although it'll keep your tastebuds awake.

Thai Streetvender's Chicken (Gai Yahng)

Directions

Use two packs of boneless, skinned chicken breasts, although this is an option—it can be done with any part of the chicken or a whole roasting chicken, whatever. Make more than enough, since this is excellent cold.

You're going to want to make a Cilantro Pesto next:

1 teaspoon freshly ground pepper. If your peppermill has a setting on it, grind the pepper as coarsely as possible. Or score coarse-ground pepper at the market.

1 cup of fresh cilantro (coriander) leaves, coarsely chopped. Thai recipes allow a lot of faking (assuming you're not having a friend from Bangkok

for dinner, who'll make rude faces), but fresh cilantro ain't one of them. Fresh or find another recipe.

2 tablespoons coarsely chopped garlic

3 tablespoons soy sauce. A digression here—if you've got the time, and are in a good-sized city, it's worthwhile scoring high-quality soy sauce. There is a difference between that and, say, Kikkoman, even though that's pretty good. Commercial plug here—a good place to get most Asian spices and such is Spice Merchant, P. O. Box 524, Jackson Hole, WY 83001. Order line: 1-800-551-5999.

1 teaspoon salt

Moosh all this stuff together, and slather it on the chicken. Let the chicken marinate in a covered plastic container (unless you *love* the smell of garlic) for anywhere from 4 hours on. If you're gonna cook this the next day, refrigerate.

Next you're going to prepare a Sweet-Hot Garlic Sauce.

1 cup sugar

½ cup water

½ cup white vinegar

1 teaspoon salt

Throw these ingredients into a saucepan and bring to a boil, stirring constantly to keep from burning the sugar. Reduce the heat to low, and let simmer for 20 minutes, until it thickens a little. Remove from the heat, and add:

2 tablespoons of chili-garlic sauce. Chili-garlic sauce is common in most Asian countries and is surprisingly available in most stores. I'd suggest, rather than using the Thai chili-garlic sauce, that you use Korean or Indonesian, which is hotter and neater and less smooth. If you can't find any sauce like that, you can fake it with a tablespoon of ground dried red chili peppers (more if you like it hotter) .

Add this to your syrup, and let cool. This'll keep for 2 or 3 weeks.

Stoke up your barbecue, and while the coals are hot, grill the chicken, dumping the remaining Pesto on it as it cooks. Let the chicken blacken a bit on the outside for a crackly skin.

With this goes:

🍴

Cucumber Pickle

½ cup water
½ cup white vinegar
½ cup sugar
1 teaspoon salt

Combine all these ingredients and bring to a boil. Remove from heat and let cool.

1 big mother cucumber, or a couple-three l'il guys, peeled and thin-sliced
4 tablespoons coarsely-chopped red onion
1 or 2 tablespoons coarsely chopped jalepeño peppers (or use any sort of
    pepper you like—habeñero if you've got big brass balls or a deathwish)
½ cup coarsely chopped fresh cilantro (coriander) leaves
¼ cup coarsely-chopped dry-roasted peanuts

Toss all this into your syrup and refrigerate. This should be made about 4 hours before you eat or, better, the day before. The same day it's good, the next day it's superior, and then it starts declining. After a week, it's not worth the bother.

With this, serve rice. You can get horrendous authentic and do Sticky Rice, which is a bastard on roller skates to do, and I'd suggest you consult a good Thai cookbook to learn how (like Nancie McDermott's *Real Thai*). For me, it ain't worth the bother. What is worthwhile is hunting down some jasmine rice, and using that instead of standard. Again, it's surprisingly easy to find in markets.

🍴

Real Mincemeat

There are people in this world who think that mincemeat doesn't contain meat, but is that sickening glop that you get in supermarkets. It ain't, and it does.

This is an old, original family recipe that dates back to, oh, last week and is utterly wonderful.

Requirements

The first thing you need is a crock. No, not the last editor who suggested you had the writing skills of a dead bat. Crocks are pottery and are available in various sizes. I've had a 5-gallon sucker for about 15 years. You can find them in *real* hardware stores (not chains) or almost all pottery outlets and stores. A smaller version is called a bean pot and is pottery with a top on it, and holds a gallon or so, and is intended for the baking of beans. Duh. It works pretty well (although see story below for possible problems). You can use crocks for not only mincemeat but to make pickles, sauerbrauten, kimchee, sauerkraut, corned beef, pickled pigs feet . . . whatever.

You will also need a meat grinder. I use the standard hand-cranked Universal #2, although if you're a high-dollar spender an electric grinder is a nifty thing to have.

Ingredients

- 2 to 3 pounds of venison. Where I live, deer is a matter of sticking your head out the back door and whistling. If you can't get venison, use the same amount of a good beef roast
- 1 fresh beef tongue, about 3 pounds
- 1 pound beef kidney suet
- 4 cups raisins
- 4 cups golden raisins
- 1 cup citron, diced
- peel of 2 large oranges, diced
- peel of 1 large lemon, diced
- 1 cup dried figs, chopped
- 3 cups sugar
- 1 teaspoon *each* of salt, cinnamon, allspice, nutmeg
- 1 quart *each* of brandy and sherry. I know they say to use the same quality booze to cook with that you drink, but in this case you can use wino-grade sherry and California brandy

Directions

Throw the venison and the tongue into a pot of water, seasoned with whatever you think is right. I'd suggest a quarter-palmful of thyme, savory, rosemary, salt, freshly ground pepper, and oregano.

Simmer these suckers for 2 hours. Yank them out of their bath and let them cool off.

Trim all surviving fat off the beef if you're using that.

Now comes the gross and disgusting part.

You'll notice the tongue looks . . . well, like what you've got lolling around in your mouth. You're going to want to skin it (the beef one, I mean), using a very sharp small knife. The tongue's outer layer cuts away easily, and can be peeled like an orange.

It really helps, during this phase of the operation, if you put on your Torquemada hat and think fondly of no-longer-loved husbands, wives, editors, agents, whatever. I personally reflect on two martial-arts stars I was unfortunate enough to work with during my Hollyweird days, but that's another story. Believe it or not, tongue is pretty good, with fresh horseradish, but that's the Swedish side of me talking, so don't pay a lot of attention. We also eat cod preserved in lye, which is *really* disgusting.

Now you're going to want to chop the roast and the tongue up into chunks large enough to fit into the mouth of the grinder (about 1- or 2-inch cubes). You'll run across li'l bitty bones in the rear of the tongue, and gristle and fat. Discard all of this crud.

Now put the cubed meat, alternating with the suet, through the grinder.

Dump all that into the crock. Dump all the rest of the ingredients in. Mix with a big wooden spoon.

Now add one quart of brandy. The mixture will suck it up like there's no tomorrow. Next add sherry until you get a slurry-like mixture. This'll take most of the sherry. Don't drink the rest of the sherry—you'll be needing this.

Cover the crock with cheesecloth and hold it in place with a big rubber band.

Let time pass. Every now and then, check it and add more booze, stirring as you do. When the sherry runs out, buy a quart of brandy. Then more sherry. And so on and so forth.

Always keep it nice and sloppy.

This mixture will live for damned near forever, unless you do something dumb (as I've done a lot) and forget to add booze or put an airtight cover on. My last batch lasted for two years.

You want to age this sucker before you make your pies. For Christmas pies, put the mixture down about Halloween—at least two months is needed for this to be good.

Now, for your pie.

Make a standard crust. Your upper crust will be interlaced strips, not a solid cover.

Combine 1 cup of the mincemeat with ¼ cup of peeled, chopped tart olives (Granny Smith are good, Newton are better). Since the booze will cook off, moisten this mixture with some Martinelli's apple juice.

Cook like a standard pie.

Serve with hard sauce (use any of the ones in *Joy of Cooking*), or you *can*, for wretched overkill, add a slice of Roquefort on top. The pie can be served hot or warmed.

Now the story that goes with this goop:

My kindly old father got bagged one day, many years ago, and decided it was time for he and my mother to make their eldest a mince pie. He was making his mincemeat—same recipe, essentially—in a bean pot. So they did. At the time, I was just finishing Advanced Infantry Training at Fort Ord. In June. About the time I finished AIT, they shipped the pie off. Unfortunately, I was at Fort Benning, going through jump school. The Army mail system punted the pie after me. It got to Fort Benning about the time I joined the 101st Airborne, at Fort Campbell, KY. About the time the pie got to Fort Campbell, I was on my way to Korea . . . by *very* slow troopship. The pie trotted along behind . . . on an even slower ship. Dissolve to December, on the Imjin River, where I was in the process of learning that a truce does *not* necessarily mean people don't shoot at you. As I recall I was trying to figure out why a .50 caliber machine gun wasn't machine-gunning when the mail clerk found me. "Bunch, you got a package. Get your butt up and get it."

"Right, okay. When I get a second."

"I mean NOW!"

Since he marginally outranked me, I shrugged and . . . and got my pie. Whooo.

In spite of the cold, the aroma traveled, like through the mailroom walls and into the Commanding Officer's office. Being a professional coward, I didn't open the package, but immediately called for an airstrike.

About the same time, all the way across the Pacific, the beanpot exploded.

Now try to tell me there ain't no such thing as the occult! This mincemeat is completely addictive, preposterously rich, guaranteed to make your fillings fall out, and shows that while our ancestors were sexist, bigoted murderers, they sometimes knew how to eat.

Mike Byers has been "a military pilot, a covert operations type, and (for ten years), actually held a more-or-less honest job with an engineering company." Since 1986, he has made most of his living with commissioned architectural stained glass, glass etching, sculpture, and kiln-worked glass pieces. He has been reading science fiction since he was six years old, but started to write it just a few years ago. His short stories have appeared in a number of magazines, including Pulphouse.

Mike Byers

⑂

Attack of the Green Bean Monster Soup

On the main, it's pretty quiet here in Warren County, Indiana. Granted, we've got Indiana's highest waterfall (sort of like having the highest mountain in Florida), the seventh biggest rock in the United States (don't bother to visit, it's mostly underground) and a tombstone that reads "Here Lies the Devil" (the coffin is empty, from what I hear). But we've also got no stoplights, fast food, hotels, motels, or 7-11 stores. It's a primitive place, so primitive (to steal a line from the late Gamble Rogers) that right-of-way is still figured to be a function of mass times velocity. Tourism is not exactly part of the local economy.

The most important thing in Warren County is real dirt. And I mean honest dirt, none of your anemic, sandy clay or gritty orange stuff that looks like it ought to be on Mars, and none of that rocky, hardscrabble misery that would just about allow five generations of farmers to stave to death, slowly. No sir, we've got the real thing: black dirt, topsoil loam twenty feet deep and so fertile that if you spit a pumpkin seed on the ground, the vine is like to grow up through our boot laces so fast that you'll be trapped there until some ody comes to cut you loose.

Real dirt can be dangerous for those who are ignorant of, or refuse to heed, Hunter's Law: "If you plant one hill of beans, they will die. If you plant ten hills of beans, they will all grow, overwhelming your garden, home and any small children or animals that happen to be playing in the yard." Being by inclination a scofflaw, I have been forced to deal with the Great Bean Monster by coming up with various recipes. The sour mash bean whiskey was not so good, I admit, and the green bean ice cream was even worse (even though it had a pleasant color) but this one, aha! This one is a winner. One caution though: this soup is supposed to taste good. It's not politically correct, and contains cream, butter and yes, even salt. If you're the sort of person who can't tolerate this sort of thing, you'd be safer to grab a load of tofu, jump in your little, bitty car with only four lug nuts on each wheel and drive right back to California. Otherwise, I won't be responsible.

Ingredients

   5 cups fresh green beans, cut into ½-inch lengths
   1 medium onion, chopped
   2 cloves garlic, finely chopped
   2 tablespoons fresh dill, chopped
   2 tablespoons butter
   1 tablespoon toasted sesame oil
   ½ teaspoon Tabasco
   ½ teaspoon freshly ground black pepper
   4 cups chicken stock
   2 cups cream or half-and-half
   salt to taste
   dill sprigs for garnish

Directions

   Sauté green beans, onion, garlic, and dill in butter and sesame oil for about 10 minutes. Add Tabasco and black pepper. Add chicken stock and simmer for about 20 minutes. Puree the soup in a blender or food processor; return to the pot and add cream (or half-and-half) and salt to taste. This can be served hot, but I think it's best when chilled for 2 or 3 hours. Garnish with a sprig of fresh dill.
   Serves 6 to 8.

Leonard Carpenter is the author of eleven Conan the Barbarian novels, most recently Conan, Lord of the Black River. This story may help explain his prolific career!

Leonard Carpenter

¶D

Rondrini's Linguini and Clam Sauce

This recipe was invented by my oldest friend Ronald Andrini, who first approached me in fourth grade by describing a dream he'd had about me. In the dream, he and I were pitted against each other in the gladiatorial arena. The Emperor ordered the arena flooded, I was vanquished, and all that remained was my glasses floating in a pool of blood.

Needless to say, we hit it off splendidly. In our subsequent gladiatorial contests, we decided that the reason our Emperor signaled "thumbs up" or "thumbs down" was that his mouth was crammed full of some thick, pasty substance, preventing speech. By diligent intuition and invention, Ron recreated the concoction that must have been the epicurean Emperor's favorite. It was later refined by my wife and myself into a palatable and, in fact delicious, cheap, and quick-cooking entree which we honor with the name, "Rondrini's Linguini."

Ingredients

2 quarts water, briskly boiling
1 tablespoon basil leaves, chopped or dry
2 tablespoons butter or olive oil
2 cloves garlic, chopped
1 (8-ounce) can chopped clams, with juice
2 tablespoons flour
4 ounces cream cheese
¼ cup milk
½ cup Parmesan or Romano cheese (dry, grated)
²/₃ pound dry linguini noodles
pepper to taste

Directions

Start water boiling for linguini. Sauté basil in butter over medium heat, then stir in garlic. Add clams with juice. Sprinkle in flour and stir until thickening begins. Add milk if a thinner sauce is desired. Add cream cheese and stir until dissolved. Then add Parmesan and stir until melted. Sauce may be served creamy or allowed to sit until thick and pasty. Serve over linguini noodles cooked al dente. Sliced zucchini sautéed in garlic and oil make an excellent side dish.

Serves 4.

Grant Carrington began publishing science fiction in 1971 and has made periodiodic forays into the field ever sinse. He is, notably, one of the authors who contributed recipes to Anne McCaffrey's first science fiction cookbook, Cooking Out of This World, *and we are delighted to welcome him back again.*

Grant Carrington

🍴

Ultimate Peanut Butter, Cream Cheese, and Onion Sandwich

It was 1964 or 1965 and Lary Wolken and I were returning from a concert at either The Showboat Lounge or Ontario Place (both now long gone, alas) in D.C. I was hungry but neither of us had a nickel. We had spent every last cent to pay the tab. (Now I remember: it was The Showboat, where we had seen Mose Allison. We were about 15 cents short but we didn't have to wash any dishes.)

Well, there wasn't much in Larry's apartment either: a half a loaf of bread, some scrapings of peanut butter, and a little bit of cream cheese. Well, why not? But as I finished putting everything on the bread, I noticed one more item, an item I never could resist, even in this context. So a couple of slices with a knife and Voila! The Peanut Butter, Cream Cheese, and Onion Sandwich was born.

I made quite a few of them in the ensuing years but have given up on them due to a rapidly increasing equator. I've only managed to convince one other person to try one. He liked it—but anyone who's dumb enough to try one probably is the kind of person who would like it. A few hints: about twice as much cream cheese as peanut butter, so the peanut butter doesn't overpower the cheese. And don't use chunky peanut butter. Otherwise you won't know if you're biting into a chunk of peanut or a piece of onion.

Since publishing his first novel, A Jungle of Stars, *in 1976, Jack Chalker has gone on to create several memorable series, including the Well World books,* The Four Lords of the Diamond, *the Quintara Marathon, and many more. But despite these works' great and lasting popularity, he may be best remembered for his exhaustive scholarship in researching and indexing small press publishers and their books. His mammoth* The Science-Fantasy Publishers: A Critical and Bibliographic History *remains one of the landmarks of science fiction scholarship. Of this recipe, he writes that it is something of a rebuttal to Ursula K. Le Guin's recipe for crabs in Anne McCaffrey's last cookbook,* Cooking Out of This World.

Jack L. Chalker

¶D

Maryland Crab Cakes

I come from a very old family by U.S. terms. The first direct Chalker ancestor arrived in Connecticut in 1639; the family wound up settling pure Yankee regions: Connecticut, upstate New York, the Lake Erie shore of Ohio, up the eastern side of Michigan's lower peninsula. All Chalkers I've ever met in the U.S. are from this grouping; none went south until a Chalker woman married a man who became governor of Georgia early in the twentieth century and hired all the relatives.

My maternal ancestors came to Tidewater, Virginia, in 1701, settling from Norfolk up the James River valley through Suffolk, then the little towns that dotted the Great Dismal Swamp like Ivor and Zuni. I myself was closer to this Hopkins-Rawls branch of the family overall than the Chalkers, and my mother and her mother determined what I grew up eating. I myself was born and raised in Maryland, right in between, but which is in its culinary tastes basically oriented to the great Chesapeake Bay that divides the state and runs from Baltimore, where I was born, to Norfolk. I am old enough to remember when overnight steamships of the Old Bay Line connected the two cities and also me and my southern relatives.

Maryland is a small state with a small population for the region. The Maryland blue crab is an amazing creature that ranges from Naragansett Bay in Rhode Island all the way down to Florida, then skips the southern tip and picks up again around Tampa Bay going all the way to Brownsville, Texas. It's a very, very different crab than most people know, although it has the usual claws and ugly disposition. It is a swimmer, with flipper-like legs, and it propels itself almost like a jet when it has to. Anyone looking for crab's legs to eat is going to be disappointed. Aside from the usual claw meat common to all edible crabs worldwide, the blue crab uniquely has all of its best meat inside the body of the crab itself. This "backfin" is considered by chefs the finest flavored shellfish meat in the world.

Maryland, a small state, eats almost half of the entire blue crab commercial catch. Crab houses are everywhere, even a hundred miles from the Bay in the mountains. Crabs, steamed live in Old Bay seasoning and served with thick Maryland crab soup, corn on the cob, and a lager beer are the common food of Marylanders at backyard picnics, and you can even order them just like pizza from ubiquitous crab houses. Since almost everyone in Maryland has been nipped by one while swimming in the Bay, even Maryland vegetarians don't consider the crustaceans meat.

Other places catch the crab and fix it in a lot of ways, but only Maryland knows how to do it right. On the other hand, anybody can create my family's legendary crab cakes if you have access in the supermarket or fish market to backfin blue crab meat. Please note that this meat should *never* be frozen. If it isn't fresh and shipped just "on ice," forget it. Also, this recipe is for backfin of the blue crab only. If you try it with any of that tasteless meat from those hollow west coast crabs, forget it. You need backfin to make this work.

Ingredients

  about 3 saltines worth of finely crumbled cracker crumbs
  1 teaspoon chopped fresh parsley
  1 pound backfin blue crabmeat, preferably select grade
  1 whole egg
  2 tablespoons mayonnaise
  salt and white pepper to taste
  dry mustard to taste
  dash Tabasco sauce

Directions

  Sprinkle cracker crumbs and parsley over crabmeat and toss lightly. In another bowl, combine egg, mayonnaise, salt, pepper, mustard, and Tabasco—beat well. Pour over crabmeat and toss lightly. When crabmeat is thoroughly mixed in with preparation, form the mixture into hamburger-size cakes and brown lightly.

  Cakes can be the basis of crab cake sandwiches adorned with dash of cocktail sauce or as the fish entree in a balanced meal. Anyone adding tartar sauce will be keelhauled.

Deborah Chester—who writes as Sean Dalton and Jay D. Blakeney—is the author of the critically acclaimed Anthi *sequence of books, including* The Children of Anthi *and* Requiem for Anthi, *although her* Operation StarHawks *adventure stories may be her best-known works.*

Deborah Chester
(Sean Dalton)

ᵲᴅ

Ham and Spaghetti

This a simple, hearty dish—great on winter evenings, especially when served with salad and homemade bread. I like to make a huge batch of it, then reheat in the microwave for quick lunch.

The recipe was invented by my best friend's great-uncle who had a farm in Missouri, and has been handed down to her father and her, then to me and my family.

The fun part of making it is letting bits of the ham stick and almost burn in the skillet. These brown bits are the secret ingredient that really gives this dish its flavor.

Ingredients

1 large onion, finely chopped
1 clove garlic, minced
2 tablespoons oil
1 pound of ham, finely chopped
2 (11½-ounce) cans Spicy & Hot V8 juice
half package spaghetti, broken into short lengths
Black ground pepper

Directions

In large skillet, sauté onion and garlic in oil until clear. Add ham and continue to cook over medium heat, stirring frequently.

Cook spaghetti in boiling water for 10 minutes, or according to package directions. Do not overcook.

When ham and onion mixture is very brown and sticking to bottom of skillet, stir in V8 juice. This will loosen all the "brown bits" stuck to the bottom of the skillet. Reduce heat and let simmer while spaghetti finishes cooking. If mixture gets too thick, add water.

Drain spaghetti and add to ham mixture. Simmer about 5 minutes, then serve.

Variations

I like to use salad macaroni instead of spaghetti, chiefly because I don't have to break it into small pieces. Any small pasta will do, even the Texas-shaped kind, although Oklahoma-shaped would be better.

This dish can be made very spicy with the garlic and black pepper, or it can be toned down to suit individual tastes.

Greg Costikyan

🍴

Pasta Puttanesca

It's always puzzled me that food doesn't play more of a role in science fiction; food tells you a lot about a culture, and food choice is an excellent way to say something about a character. And a great deal of social life in all cultures occurs over food. Food does appear prominently in most of my work; and understandably. Science fiction and games are now professional pursuits for me, so cooking is one of my few remaining hobbies.

In any event, everyone should have a good Puttanesca in his or her repertoire; it's simple, extraordinarily tasty, and is prepared mainly with canned ingredients, meaning you can have the necessaries on hand at all times in case the unexpected extraterrestrial should drop in and require feeding. Better a plate of pasta than you, or the cat.

"Puttanesca" means "whore-style." The claim is that it's cheap and tasty and was popular with streetwalkers in Rome as a result.

Ingredients

2 large cloves garlic, chopped
1 can of anchovies
1 (28-ounce) can of Italian-style peeled tomatoes
1 pound pasta (ziti is best)
2 tablespoons olive oil
$^1/_8$ teaspoon red pepper flakes
¼ cup capers (the cheaper Spanish capers are preferable to the more
    expensive nonpareils)
½ cup black olives (buy and the deli counter and pit yourself—canned
    work, but they're far less tasty)
black pepper to taste
¼ cup fresh parsley, chopped

Directions

Set a pot of water to boil for the pasta; add salt to taste. A little oil floating on the surface will help keep the pasta from sticking.

Chop the garlic and open the anchovies. Pour off the oil from the anchovies and chop coarsely.

Open the can of tomatoes, and pour off the liquid. Squeeze the individual tomatoes to extract the liquid caught inside. Roughly chop the squeezed tomatoes.

At about this point, put the pasta into the boiling water. Stir briskly; from now until the pasta is ready, stir frequently to prevent it from sticking. Do not overcook; keep the pasta al dente.

Heat the olive oil in a frying pan. Add the garlic and red pepper flakes; swirl a bit, then add the anchovies and smush with a fork until the anchovies dissolve in the oil. (Do fish dissolve? Yes, in this case they do.)

Add the chopped tomatoes and mix thoroughly. Add the capers, black olives and black pepper to taste. You probably don't need to add salt; the anchovies and capers are salty enough. Stir and reduce the heat so the sauce will simmer, but not overcook.

Shortly before the pasta is done, add the chopped parsley and stir.

Drain the pasta. You may mix with the sauce, or serve the sauce separately. Puttanesca is traditionally served without cheese, but I prefer a bit of freshly grated Romano or Parmesan nonetheless.

Incidentally, if you omit the black olives and add a can of tuna and a bit of tomato paste, you have a very nice Pasta al Tonno.

🍴

Glace "Doc" Smith

To make ice cream, you must a) freeze the mixture, and b) aerate it. You can do this in a traditional ice cream freezer, which both cools the mixture and whips it, mixing bubbles of air into it as it freezes. You can also do it by pouring liquid nitrogen into the mixture. The liquid nitrogen freezes it—and, as the liquid becomes a gas, aerates it as well. I've seen this demonstrated, but have never actually done it myself. However, I present the recipe below for your enjoyment. I'm naming it after E. E. "Doc" Smith, author of the Lensman saga—and a food scientist.

Requirements

> large stainless steel bowl
> ceramic heat plates
> heavy tongs
> face shield
> protective mitts

Ingredients

> 4 egg yolks
> ½ cup sugar
> 1 cup milk
> ⅔ cup heavy cream
> 1 large vanilla bean
> 1 liter liquid nitrogen
> ½ teaspoon vanilla
> extra pinch of salt

Directions

Cream the egg yolks and sugar together.

Mix the milk and cream in a saucepan. Slice the vanilla bean in half lengthwise and discard the seeds; add it to the milk. Cook the milk over a low fire, stirring constantly, until it begins to steam (but not to boil).

Remove the vanilla bean.

Add the egg yolk and sugar mixture to the saucepan, little by little, whisking it vigorously into the mixture. Continue cooking until the custard is quite thick.

Allow the mixture to cool. While it is doing so, slice the vanilla bean into tiny pieces and return it to the mixture. Pour the mixture into the stainless steel bowl. Place it on the ceramic heat plates.

Open the flask of liquid nitrogen. Don the face shield and protective gloves. Take the flask of liquid nitrogen with the tongs, and pour it slowly into the stainless steel bowl.

When the "steam" has cleared, you will have ice cream. (You probably don't need to use the full liter.)

You can substitute any ice cream mixture.

Yields 4 cups.

Melissa Crandall has been writing stories since she was seven, but professionally only since 1991. Her musical tastes cover a wide range from classical to Celtic New Grass. Her hero is Jane Goodall. She likes spending far too much money at library book sales and buying old furniture and then thinking about refinishing it. Currently, her favorite film is Braveheart, *and* not *because of Mel Gibson (though no one believes her). She lives somewhere in the Continental United States (precisely where that's going to be is an issue up in the air as of this writing) with her husband, Ed, and three entertaining felines: Baroness Ripley Von Schnorten-Blorter, Miss Curie Pigger-Lumpton, and Yeti the Abominable Snowcat. She's proud to be a card-carrying Wicked Stepmother, and thinks her stepkids are nifty people.*

Melissa Crandall

ᵟᴰ

Depressed Clam Chowder

My grandmother, Geneva Shorey Crandall Sherman Burton (whew!) made this dish to get her six hungry children through the Depression in Oakfield, Maine. Gram is gone, but the recipe lives on as it was given to me, plain and unadulterated. Like me, you'll have to devise your own proportions for your particular household.

Ingredients

Chopped raw potatoes (Skins on or off, as you prefer. My mother guessti-
mates about one quart for every can of clams used, but it's really up to
personal preference.)
1 to 2 chopped onions
1 to 2 cans evaporated milk
clams (however much it takes to make it "clammy" enough for you) and
juice, if canned

Directions

Put potatoes and onions into soup pot. Add enough water to just cover them. Cook until potatoes are tender, but not mushy. Add evaporated milk and clams. Heat through and serve.

Note: This is a thin-brothed chowder that can always be thickened as you would a gravy, or by pureeing part of the batch before adding the clams. This is great on its own, fine with crackers, and heavenly with a slab of fresh-baked bread.

⑩

Eric's Veggie Pie

During my single semester at Southampton College on Long Island, I met Eric Halter, a geology undergraduate. He took me on tours of everything from the walking dunes to the beaches and jetties. During one such foray, I broke a toe. It was a small break, but very painful and luridly purple. To make up for it, Eric hobbled me back to his house and baked this pie. All in all, it was a nice way to round out the day (barring that his kitten, Merlin, chose to piddle on me.) Nowadays, I'm on the East Coast and Eric is in Hawaii, but every time I make this I think of him.

Ingredients

1½ cups milk
½ cup flour
2 to 3 eggs
pinch of salt and pepper
2 cups broccoli or cauliflower, chopped
½ cup onion, chopped
½ cup green pepper, chopped
1 cup cheddar cheese, shredded

Directions

Blend milk, flour, eggs, salt, and pepper until smooth. Stir in remaining ingredients and pour into greased casserole or pie pan. Bake 35 to 40 minutes at 400 degrees or until a knife comes cleanly out of the center. This makes about 4 servings and, really, any veggie combination can be used.

🍴

Pouch Dinners

Created in a rushed moment of inspiration when a deadline demanded I be at the computer, but there were hungry mouths waiting to be fed.

Ingredients per pouch

a few slices of onion
1 hamburger patty
1 to 2 carrots, cut into chunks
1 potato, halved or quartered
a few slices of green pepper
1 to 2 stalks of celery, cut into chunks
¼ (or slightly more) cup stewed tomatoes
salt and pepper to taste

Directions

On a sheet of aluminum foil, with the sides brought up and secured to form a pouch, put a slice or two of onion, the hamburger patty, and the rest of the ingredients. Seal pouch, put on baking tray, and bake at 375 degrees for 1 hour or until veggies are done.

🍴

"Pull My Finger" Carrot Cake

Some of you will know to what this name refers and the rest of you should praise your ignorance. Suffice to say that my husband, who is in the navy, has a best friend (also in the navy) who can be singularly disgusting at times. This cake (which is *not* disgusting except, perhaps, disgustingly rich) is named for him.

Ingredients

2 cups sugar
2 teaspoon cinnamon
2 cups flour
½ teaspoon salt
2 teaspoons baking soda

1 cup oil
4 eggs
3 cups grated carrots
1 cup shredded coconut
1 cup chopped walnuts

Directions

Preheat oven to 350 degrees. In one bowl, mix sugar, cinnamon, flour, salt, and baking soda. In another bowl, mix oil and eggs. Add this to dry ingredients and blend well. Add carrots, coconut, and nuts, and mix well. Pour into greased 9 x 13-inch pan and bake for 35 to 40 minutes.

🍴

Chocolate Chip Cookies

I once had a young man in Viking garb propose to me after eating one of these cookies. (I turned him down, but it was a nice compliment.)

Ingredients

2¼ cups flour
1 teaspoon baking soda
1 teaspoon salt (optional)
1 cup butter, softened (unsalted is best, or leave out additional salt*)
¼ cup sugar
¼ cup packed brown sugar
1 teaspoon vanilla
½ teaspoon water
2 eggs
½ package semisweet chocolate chips
½ package peanut butter chips

Directions

Preheat oven to 375 degrees. In small bowl, mix flour, baking soda, and salt. In large bowl, mix butter, sugars, vanilla, and water. Add eggs and mix well. Add flour mixture. Add chips. Drop by the spoonful onto a cookie sheet. Bake 10 to 12 minutes.

Kate Daniel moved to Arizona in search of mountains and wide horizons. She found them and hasn't tired of them in the twenty-plus years since then. Author of several mystery novels for young adults, Kate has also appeared in a number of SF anthologies. She has just completed another mystery and is at work on her first science fiction novel.

Kate Daniel

ℹ️

3C Soup

When I first created this, I was stuck for a name. Then I looked at the fact that it's got chicken broth, celery, and cucumber, et voila! 3C Soup.

The name has a fine skiffy ring to it. If they want to serve it on an interstellar liner, they may do so with my blessings, but they have to let me deadhead with them. And they have to give me a credit line on the menu.

Since this was created during an Arizona summer, when the air outside is *hot*, it's a cold soup. Cold soups are a delight on a summer day. Of course, this means there are four Cs in the soup, but I didn't think that sounded quite as good. So call it *cold* 3C Soup, if you will.

Ingredients

1 bunch celery
1 large sweet onion
chicken broth
peeled cucumber
½ teaspoon dill weed
1 cup good plain yoghurt

Directions

Clean and chop one entire bunch of celery and one large sweet onion. Place in a saucepan with just enough chicken broth to cover, and cook until falling-apart tender. Let cool.

Drain the celery and onion, reserving the liquid. Using a blender or food processor, liquify the celery and onion with an equal amount of raw peeled cucumber and dill weed. Add the reserved broth until the mixture is the consistency you want. Strain to remove fiberous bits. Stir in one cup of *good* plain yoghurt, preferably homemade. (For a variation, substitute sour cream for the yoghurt.) Chill till icy-cold.

To serve, garnish each bowlful (or the tureen) with a spoonful of sour cream or yoghurt sprinkled with chopped chives, fresh dill weed, or black pepper. Serve with good bread and butter and a green salad for a summer supper. (Also makes a *great* dish for potlucks!)

🍴

Marco Polo Chicken Salad

This is a new one, created after I first heard about the cookbook. Once I tried it and it worked, I knew I had to offer it to the cookbook as well.

One of the inventions Marco Polo brought back from the orient was noodles. Since then, his homeland of Italy has been associated with pasta in many forms. So what would *you* call a recipe that's both Italian and Chinese?

Except of course it isn't Chinese and it isn't Italian. It comes from an American kitchen, as the melting pot does its thing again. But I think anyone who likes Chinese food and macaroni will enjoy this.

Ingredients

1 (12-ounce) package of elbow or similar macaroni
3 chicken breasts
2 cups chicken broth
2 small onions, sliced thin
4 cloves of garlic, slivered
4 crushed red chili pods
4 dried tomatoes
2 tablespoons cornstarch
1 teaspoon brown sugar
½ teaspoon powdered ginger
1 tablespoon red wine vinegar
1 tablespoon soy sauce
Optional: almonds, water chestnuts, diced celery, bean sprouts, bamboo
   shoots

Directions

Cook, rinse, drain, and cool one 12-ounce package of elbow or similar macaroni.

Simmer 3 chicken breasts in chicken broth, along with 2 small onions sliced thin, 4 slivered cloves of garlic, 4 crushed red chili pods, and 4 dried tomatoes. When the chicken is cooked to the bone, remove and cool. Let the liquid reduce by half. When it is reduced, mix cornstarch, brown sugar, and powdered ginger with red wine vinegar and soy sauce. Use to thicken the sauce. When thick, remove and cool. Dice the meat and the dried tomatoes and return to the sauce.

Combine macaroni and sauce with almonds, water chestnuts, diced celery, a can of bean sprouts, and bamboo shoots if desired. Mix well and chill. Makes bunches, with good leftovers.

This is an excerpt from The Peasant Cookbook, *which has been an ongoing project for some years. As to the authors, Avram Davidson (1923–1993) was one of the science fiction and fantasy field's unique voices, and his novels included such classics as* The Phoenix and the Mirror *and* Vergil in Avernus. *His friend and sometime collaborator (and an accomplished author in her own right), Grania Davis, is executor of his literary estate, wrapping up many projects left unfinished or unsold. One recent accomplishment is the upcoming publication of a "Best of Avram Davidson" short story collection from* White Wolf.

Avram Davidson and Grania Davis

¶D

Pa's Peasant Soup

How nice the bakery smelled when they were bringing out the fresh rolls, tumbling them from the heavy wire trays into the bins in the showcase. The rolls were round and brown and so crisp and they had poppy seeds all over the top. They came off, the poppy seeds, while the rolls were tumbling out, and they came off in the brown paper bags the customers took them home in, and they came off on the tablecloth while the rolls were being spread with sweet butter. But there were always enough left on, the crisp brown crust broken open to the sweet white insides, up to the last bite. Nothing wasted.

Ingredients

1½ pounds lean beef or veal shank, or other stewing cut with bones
1 soup chicken (free range, if you can find it!) all fat removed
2 to 3 quarts water (enough to cover all the ingredients, but not overflow
    your soup pot. You can add more as the soup boils down.)
2 tender leeks, trimmed and sliced (or one sweet onion)
2 or 3 fresh carrots, trimmed and sliced
2 celery stalks (with leaves), sliced
2 young turnips, cut into chunks
1 whole unpeeled small new potato per person
2 tablespoon chopped parsley
1 tablespoon chopped dill
2 teaspoons salt (you can always put it in, but you can't take it out!)
2 teaspoons coarse ground pepper

1 bay leaf
2 cloves minced garlic (more or less)
1 cup dry white wine (more or less)
2 cups chopped cabbage
1 cup sliced mushrooms

Directions

Quickly sear and brown the beef or veal on the bottom of a big soup pot. Add the cut up chicken and 2 quarts of water. Bring to a boil, then simmer for 1 hour and skim off any excess fat and foam. Add the leeks, carrots, celery, turnips, potatoes, seasonings, and wine, and more water if needed. Bring to a boil, then simmer for 30 minutes. Add the cabbage and mushrooms, and more water or seasoning if needed. Simmer another 30 minutes or until everything is tender but not mushy.

Serve it in big soup bowls. Give everyone a piece of chicken, a piece of meat, a whole new potato, and plenty of broth and vegetables. A plate of horseradish or mustard on the side can serve as a dipping sauce. Serves 4 to 6, and makes great leftovers.

The only side dish you need are round and brown and crispy rolls with poppy seeds and sweet butter.

Author Nicholas DiChario instructs a writers workshop at Writers & Books, a non-profit literary organization in Rochester, New York. The course is entitled Surrealistic Fudge and is designed to encourage beginning writers to be creative and follow their instincts and imaginations and pretty much get crazy on paper. He serves this fudge to his class. So far they've all survived.

Nicholas A. DiChario

❦

Surrealistic Fudge

The recipe is not at all complicated and has been in the family for many years. I learned it from my mother, Josephine, sans the white chocolate. (Actually, according to Mom, white chocolate was not an easily accessible ingredient years ago.) The white chocolate was added specifically for my class. It's a spiritual sort of thing, mixing the light and dark chocolate, the yin and yang, and it gives the fudge a milk-chocolatey appearance and a wonderful taste. I want my students to learn that mixing stuff in recipes or in fiction can work, as long as you've got good ingredients.

Ingredients

4½ cups sugar
1 large can evaporated milk
1 (15-ounce) white chocolate bar
12 ounces semisweet chocolate chips
7 ounces marshmallow creme
1½ teaspoons salt
1 teaspoon vanilla

Directions

Bring sugar and evaporated milk to a boil in an average-size saucepan or pot.

Cook for 5 minutes at a bubble, and stir continuously to avoid sticking.

Break white chocolate into a separate bowl (pieces should be about the size of a nickel or dime).

Add chocolate chips, marshmallow creme, salt, and vanilla.

Pour hot sugar/milk into bowl and stir all ingredients until well mixed.

Pour into 9 x 13-inch pan, cover loosely with tin foil, and refrigerate overnight.

Recipe makes approximately 5 pounds of soft-batch fudge. For hard-batch Surrealistic Fudge, add in 1 cup of chopped nuts (your choice) and increase sugar to 5 cups.

David Drake, the creator of Hammer's Slammers *and many other science fiction novels, was born in Dubuque, Iowa, in 1945. He received a B.A. in history and Latin from the University of Iowa, and a J.D. from Duke Law School in 1972. He adds, "I've worked at a variety of jobs, including a year as an interrogator in Viet Nam and Cambodia; eight years as Assistant Town Attorney for the Town of Chapel Hill, NC; and a year driving a Chapel Hill city bus (in that order). Since 1981 I've been a full-time freelance writer.*

"My wife is a simply wonderful cook, but she doesn't write."

David Drake

🍴

Pig Picking

Absolutely the only cooking I do is a pig-picking in late September for my birthday. I've got a simple iron grate on six post legs. I lean sheet metal around the sides to close it—aluminum roofing for the long sides. This *isn't* fancy. Another sheet of metal, cardboard, or even a tarp lies over the pig.

The pig is just that, a whole—approximately 100 pounds—hog, split up the middle. Unless you've got a larger cooler than mine to transport it and store it the night before, you'll probably have the head removed and maybe the trotters as well.

I get up about six in the morning and build a fire in an open-topped 55-gallon drum with a shovel hole cut in the bottom. There's holes punched about 18 inches up so that 3 iron pipes can be thrust through. They hold the larger logs to burn out of the way of the shovel with which you remove coals.

Start with the pig flesh-side down on the grate. Shake the barrel and jab the shovel down into it to knock off coals. Shovel them under the pig on the grate. (Don't build a fire directly under the pig.)

You can do the whole job with hardwood, but it'll take a lot of wood. I've come to the system of keeping a hardwood fire going, but dumping part-bags of charcoal into the bottom of the barrel to preheat and ignite. (If you put cold charcoal under the pig, it'll cool the system down before it ignites.)

I have the barrel and grate on a gravel drive. Don't have the barrel too close to the eaves of your house, and it's a good idea to have a charged hose handy while the process continues. Also, don't wear anything you mind getting spark-holes burned into. That includes your own bare skin.

Flip the pig skin-side down about noon. This takes two people and a certain amount of swearing. Baste heavily with barbeque sauce. A friend, writer Karl Wagner, traditionally made mine. It was different each year but always very hot. The base is vinegar, red pepper, and jalapeños, but there are exotics at whim. The sauce in 1993, which was wonderful, included Indian Lime Pickle. Since Karl's death, I had to start experimenting myself for my fiftieth this year.

The tenderloin should be ready to eat when you flip the pig. When it's my pig, the cook and early guests whittle it out with their pocket knives. I can't tell you how good it tastes.

Depending on variables like the weather, the pig may be ready to carve anywhere from 4 to 8 P.M. Rain will cool the air and the top sheet, greatly slowing the process.

When the pig's done, slide it onto a carving table of some sort and cut it onto platters. Removing a well-cooked pig is tricky, because it'll tend to stick to the grate and fall apart as you pull. A couple shovels and several helpers are useful. Also friends who don't complain when half the pig falls onto the gravel.

Have pitchers of sauce available for those who want more. If it's been a cool day, you may want to put the hams back on the fire for a time.

It's really not tricky, though I've learned a lot of refinements over the twenty-odd years I've been doing this. Most of them are a matter of location, available materials, and taste. There's a fairly short learning curve, and it really is a nice centerpiece to a party.

Diane Duane is the author of a score of novels of science fiction and fantasy, among them the New York Times *best-sellers* Spock's World *and* Dark Mirror, *as well as the very popular Wizard series. She lives with her husband, Peter Morwood—with whom she has written five novels, including* The Romulan Way—*in a beautiful valley in rural Ireland.*

Diane Duane and Peter Morwood

ⅅ

The Parable of the Cow and the Sofa

Sayeth Diane Duane, by way of introduction: "Some years ago, the British National Science Fiction Convention (otherwise known as Eastercon, since that's when it's routinely scheduled) was held in St. Helier in Jersey. The occasion was marked out, among other things, by the excellence of its food: the Sunday afternoon banquet was of such high quality that the chef was called out by the attendees to receive a standing ovation. (The chef in question was also a vegetarian, and his veggie entrees were so good that those who had asked for the vegetarian option were seen fighting to keep the carnivores out of their dinners.)

"Peter was asked by the convention's committee to stand up after dinner and entertain the masses. He decided that, since it was Easter, it would be appropriate for him to preach on some biblical text or another, and wound up manufacturing the text as well as the sermon based on it. A different version of 'The Parable of the Cow and the Sofa' appears in a book called *Vicarage Allsorts*, the name of whose author I can't recall at the moment. Peter made some changes to this text and then enclosed it in a longer, pseudobiblical dissertation, which went down well with the sated audience.

"When we were asked to be the ToastMr. and Mrs. at Worldcon in Glasgow, both of us plunged around for some time trying to work out exactly what we were going to do for the much larger and possibly more demanding audience present at a Hugo Awards ceremony. Only very late in the process (the night before, in fact) did it occur to us to revive this material, make certain changes reflecting the locale and the audience, and present it again, with additions—specifically, the image of a fannish dinner staged in a slightly Biblical context. It seems to have gone over okay . . ."

Today's lesson is taken from the Epistle of St. Jude the Illegible to the Glaswegians. Glaswegians three, Partick Thistle nil, verses 9 to 54 . . .

9. And it came to pass that the Lord and the disciples were at supper.

10. And they said one unto another, "This is a better supper than the last supper, for verily the oil in which they have fried the chips and the french fries thereof has been changed within the last month."

11. And they were well content, even with the deep-fried pizza. But lo, when the bill came, then they began to bicker, yea, and to squabble among themselves, saying, "I never ordered that"; and "Behold, they have overcharged us for the battered sausages"; and "They never brought my salad"; and "All right, who had the Irn-Bru?"

12. And the Lord said, "Verily, I knew this would happen: we should have stuck to loaves and fishes."

13. And to the disciples he spake, saying, "Peace, be still, and cast not the breadrolls, neither flick each other any more with the napkins.

15. "For I say unto you, I shall take this one on My Imperial Express Card.

16. "Yea, verily, unto My card they shall put the charge thereof."

17. Then the disciples were ashamed, and let fall the breadrolls, and Simon the Inebriate said, "Lord, tell us a story."

18. And the Lord said, "Anything to keep you quiet.

19. "Just give Me time to think of one."

20. And he took a cup, and raised it, and lo! that cup was empty.

21. Verily, there was no wine within that cup, yea, not even the small sticky bit like jam right at the bottom.

22. And the disciples said, "Lord, there is no wine."

23. And He said, "You lot are just like My mother."

24. And He causéd beer instead, to show them.

25. And He took that beer, and blessed it, saying, "Good, beer," and drank it to refresh His mouth withal.

26. Then wiped He the froth from His moustache, yea, from his moustache did He wipe it, and He said, "Are you all sitting comfortably?"

27. And the disciples answered, "Yea."

28 And He said, "Then I will begin."

29. And the Lord spake, saying, "There was once a man who went forth into the fields."

30. And the disciples said, "Lord, you told us that one last week."

33. Then the Lord did pause, and made consultation of His notes, and said, "Verily, it was last week in Jerusalem.

34. "Then I will tell you another one, not like the other one."

35. And they answered, "Tell us another one, do."

36. And he spake, saying, "Once there was a man who had a house, and by that house he had a field."

37. And one of the disciples said, "Is this the one about the lilies of the field and the splendor thereof?"

38. And the Lord said, "Who is telling this, thee or Me?"

39. And that disciple was silent.

40. Then the Lord said, "And in that field there dwelt a cow, yea, in that field a cow had made its residence.

41. "And it came to pass that the man went forth from his house and traveled unto a show, and there he bought a sofa: yea, a sofa purchaséd he it.

43. "And that sofa brought he unto his house, and from his house he bare it to the field.

44. "Then came the cow unto the sofa, and she sate upon it.

45. "And the man waxed wroth.

46. "Angered was he to see the cow upon his sofa, and irritable was his manner.

47. "And the man spake unto that cow, saying, 'Why sittest thou upon my sofa in this field which is mine also?'

48. "And the cow said, 'Wherefore puttest thou a sofa in my field, for verily I was in this field before the sofa?'"

49. And the Lord drank beer and was content.

50. And the disciples said, "Lord, is that it?"

51. And the Lord said, "That is it."

52. Then He went forth and walked to and fro upon the pool that was in the courtyard, which, being empty, impressed no-one.

53. But the disciples whispered privily each unto the other, saying, "Sometimes he tells good stories, but I suppose everyone is entitled to an off day, and besides, he is paying for dinner."

54. Then Simon the Inebriate rose from beneath the table and cried in a great voice, "Jedi, Jedi, Eddy Murphy!" which is to say, "I suppose you had to be there."

Here endeth the lesson.

Linda Dunn says that the best thing that happened in 1995 was her nomination for the John W. Campbell Award. "While I didn't win, it was an honor to be nominated. It was also a thrilling experience as I'd entered science fiction through the back door of fandom. I'm a member of the Circle of Janus Science Fiction Club and attended several conventions before going to my first WorldCon in Chicago a few years ago." She recently returned to college to obtain a second degree, this time majoring in Computer Science and Mathematics. Currently she lives in Indiana with her husband, Greg, and her two children, David and Toni.

Linda Dunn

ᵀĐ

Noodles with Beef Broth

Ingredients

   5 egg yolks (save egg whites for angel food cake)
   10 tablespoons beef broth
   $^1/_8$ teaspoon salt
   dash of pepper (may be omitted)
   2½ cups flour
   1 cheap cut of beef, baked at 300 degrees for about 2 hours

Directions

   Add yolks, beef broth, salt, and pepper and stir. Add flour gradually, stirring with fork. Place mixture on pastry cloth and roll thin. Let dough dry for 3 to 5 hours. Cut into noddle-sized strips. Now you've made your own—boil as with regular, store-bought noodles whenever you want them.

   I suggest covering the dough with waxed paper if you own cats. Last time I left the dough uncovered and walked away, I returned to find paw prints and cat hair all over the dough. Although the cats all had that "who me?" innocent look, I noticed that a few of them had light dustings of flour upon their paws.

   The wax paper doesn't keep the cats from walking on the dough but it does keep the cat hair out of the noodles.

Phyllis Eisenstein has been writing professionally since 1971, both on her own and in collaboration with her husband, Alex. Her novels include Born to Exile, Shadow of Earth, In the Hands of Glory, The Crystal Palace, *and* In the Red Lord's Reach—*as well as some three dozen shorter works. She has been nominated twice each for the Hugo and Nebula Awards in short fiction categories, and one of her fantasy novels,* Sorcerer's Son, *is considered a classic in the field. Ms. Eisenstein has a B.A. in anthropology and teaches science fiction writing at Columbia College of Chicago. Most recently her work appeared in the* Oxford Book of Fantasy.

Phyllis Eisenstein

🍴

Hoisin-Marinated Pork Chops

Ingredients

4 pork chops, about 1^1/$_3$ pounds total weight
Some ground black pepper
And for the marinade:
  2 tablespoons hoisin sauce (available at oriental grocery stores)
  ¼ cup white wine
  ¼ cup water
  ¼ teaspoon garlic powder
  a couple dashes of ground black pepper

Directions

The chops should be cold from the refrigerator or store. Pierce them deeply with a fork half a dozen times on each side. Mix the marinade. Put the chops in it, wetting them thoroughly on both sides. Marinate for 30 minutes, unrefrigerated, turning a couple of times.

Remove the chops from the marinade and place on a broiler rack. Sprinkle on one side with more pepper. Let them sit while you strain the marinade through a small sieve into a small saucepan. Bring the marinade to a simmer and, stirring frequently, reduce till slightly thickened.

Broil the chops on both sides. Serve with the reduced marinade as a dipping sauce. Serves 2 or 4, depending on your attitude toward pork chops.

My husband Alex and I fell in love with hoisin sauce when I began cooking Szechuan some years ago, and we've been experimenting with it ever since. If you like the flavor, hoisin works great on broiled chicken, too, either as the above marinade or as straight hoisin diluted with an equal amount of water (because it's very concentrated) and brushed on during the last 5 or 10 minutes of cooking, like barbecue sauce (or both).

ⅅ
Auntie Anne's Sweet and Sour Meatballs

Ingredients

3 pounds lean ground beef
1 medium green (bell) pepper, chopped fine
1 medium onion, chopped fine
3 eggs
1 can beef consomme
1 (12 ounce) can frozen lemonade
1½ cups tomato juice
1 cup water
4 tablespoons corn starch mixed with ⅓ cup water

Directions

In a very large bowl, mix ground beef, green pepper, onion, and eggs thoroughly and make small meatballs (an inch or so in diameter). In a large soup pot, bring consomme, lemonade, tomato juice, and water to a boil. Drop the meatballs in one by one, making sure the liquid continues to simmer the whole time. Stir gently now and then. Lower the heat and let the meatballs simmer, covered, for 20 to 30 minutes.

Turn the heat off to let the liquid stop moving. Skim the fat (there shouldn't be a lot if you used lean beef). Bring the liquid back up to a simmer and add the corn starch/water mixture. Stir gently till mixed thoroughly. When the liquid is thickened (a few minutes), the meatballs are done. Serve over rice or noodles.

My Auntie Anne first showed me how to make this dish when I was about twelve. We had to feed some two dozen people at a Passover seder, and this was the appetizer. Auntie Anne, never one to skimp on food, had doubled or maybe tripled the recipe (she was very approximate when it came to cooking); certainly, she and I seemed to be making meatballs for hours, while the rest of the meal was in the oven or on its way to her house in the hands of other relatives. We weren't even halfway through the meat mixture when the meatballs threatened to overflow the pot (her largest), so she poured some of the liquid into another pot, and we started on that. When the second one was full, we moved on to a third. By the time we were done, every burner on the stove had a pot of meatballs on it. There was, as I recall, one small plastic container's worth left at the end of the meal, and as a reward for being apprentice cook, I got to take that home.

Ru Emerson was raised in Butte, Montana in the1950s (which explains a lot) and eventually moved to Los Angeles, where she lived in some of the more "colorful" neighborhoods (Hollywood, Venice Beach, East L.A.) for "way too many years." She now lives on five wooded acres in the foothills of the Oregon Coast Range with the infamous Doug, several cats, and at least fifty flower beds. When not actually working on a book, she can be found hiking, biking, gardening or playing a character role in the local melodrama theater. Her novels include the six-volume Night-Threads series, the Nedao Trilogy, The Princess of Flames, Spellbound, and (as Roberta Cray), The Sword and the Lion. Her work has been translated into Spanish, Italian, Russian, Chinese, and German.

Ru Emerson
(Roberta Cray)

🍴

Chili Quilas

My mother (a Kansas meat-and-potatoes woman, married to a male ditto) discovered this combination when my dad was stationed in Corpus Christi, Texas, just after World War II. Her version used a bell pepper instead of chilis, no olives, no corn, Fritos, and (shudder) Velveeta. Doug and I played with this for years and have come up with a version that is fast to fix and clean up, filling, half-way nutritious, and just the item after an afternoon of tobogganing in the front yard.

Ingredients

One can chili with beans (or 2 cups of homemade)
3 to 6 ounces tomato sauce
1 can whole-kernel corn (or one 16-ounce bag frozen)
1 small can diced green chilis
1 small can sliced black olives
your choice of cheddar or other cheese for topping
corn chips, tortilla chips, Fritos—or a French bread, halved and hollowed
    out

Directions

Combine the canned ingredients in a saucepan; heat. Pour over chips or into French bread, top with sliced or shredded cheese, heat in 350-degree oven until cheese melts.

ᵗ🍴

Fettucini á là Marshall

Besides being allergic to half the "good" things to eat, I'm fussy about what I eat. When the attorney I worked for some years ago in Los Angeles invited us to dinner, Doug eyed the white sauce dubiously; he was sure there wasn't anything in there I'd eat. I didn't think so, either, until I smelled it simmering. This became our "celebration" dinner, saved for special occasions only.

Ingredients

1 pound mushrooms
1 tablespoon butter
1 pound Italian sausage (I used plain for my own sauce and give Doug my mushrooms)
1 pint whipping cream
dollop of white wine
your choice of Italian herbs (I used a homegrown blend of rosemary, thyme, basil, a touch of sage—but the grocery store bottle of dried mix will do)
8 ounces gruyere cheese (as a substitute if you live 20 miles from the nearest deli, Bonbell will do fine)

Directions

Sauté the mushrooms in butter, cook the sausage, set both aside. In sauté pan, combine cream, wine, herbs; cook on low until it bubbles; cut or break cheese into small bits, stir until cheese melts and mixture thickens. Add mushrooms and sausage, pour over and mix with pasta. This doesn't need anything but salad and bread for goeswith.

Nancy Etchemendy

🍴

Basque Potatoes with Wine

Far back in the mists of time, when women took their husbands' names more or less without asking questions, I married a dashing young Basque whose surname (Etchemendy, which means "mountain home") was almost as beautiful as his biceps. You might reasonably assume that my arcane knowledge of a dish such as Basque Potatoes with Wine is directly connected with this event. Not so. Life is always more convoluted than a reasonable person expects.

I was putting the dashing young Basque through graduate school, and we were poor. Since potatoes only cost a few cents a pound, we ate a lot of them. We ate potatoes baked and fried and scalloped and boiled; we ate them stuffed and as stuffing.

Eventually, I reached that ever-dangerous point at which I became bored with them. As any writer can tell you, the mother of invention is not really necessity. It is boredom. And it was boredom that caused me to tear the twist-cap from a bottle of jug wine (we always had plenty since it was almost as cheap as Idaho russets) and splash it recklessly into the frying pan with the spuds. The result was delicious. I thought, as I have so often before and since, that I had given birth to a wholly original idea. So it was with great pleasure and even a certain gloating that I refined the recipe over the years until family and friends came to regard it as a specialty of mine.

Time passed, and soon it was no longer fashionable to share the name of one's husband. Nevertheless, I kept Etchemendy, for it is a truly beautiful name and besides, I had by then been an Etchemendy for so long that I could barely imagine myself answering to anything else. But I kept meeting people who assumed that since I had a Basque name I must be Basque, and they would ask me embarrassing questions about Hemingway and car bombs and whether

I personally knew any revolutionaries. And I would be forced to explain that I was only Basque by osmosis.

The whole thing bothered me so much that I finally took action. Although I could never regale the curious with firsthand accounts of counter-revolutionary activities, I could at least learn Basque cooking. One day while leafing through books on the cuisine of the Pyrenees, I discovered a horrible thing. "Potatoes with Wine" was first invented in the seventeenth century by a Basque Franciscan monk whose recipe was basically the same as mine. I had been cooking Basque food for years without even realizing it. I felt just the way I did when I discovered that I was not the first person to write a story about sexually aggressive trees. Perhaps there is no such thing as a wholly original idea.

Ingredients

     5 tablespoons olive oil
     2 cloves garlic
     1 small onion, peeled and sliced thin
     garlic salt to taste
     5 medium potatoes, peeled and sliced thin
     ground pepper to taste
     4 tablespoons fresh parsley, finely chopped
     ½ cup reasonably dry white wine

Directions

Heat the olive oil in a 12-inch skillet on medium-high heat. Peel the garlic and mash it with the side of a broad chopping knife. Sauté the garlic and onion in the olive oil until the onion is transparent and just beginning to brown. Push the onions to the sides of the pan and add a layer of sliced potatoes to cover the bottom. Salt and pepper the layer of potatoes and sprinkle with parsley. Then add another layer of potatoes, parsley, and seasonings. Continue in this way till all the potatoes are used. (You should have about 3 layers when finished.) Then scoop the onions from the sides of the skillet onto the top of the potatoes. Fry the potatoes and onions till tender. Turn them every 4 or 5 minutes—the pan must he hot enough to brown the potatoes on the bottom. When all the potatoes are cooked through and some are brown and slightly crispy, pour the wine over them. (I use white because I prefer its lighter flavor. The Franciscan monk used Bordeaux, which is particularly nice if you plan to serve the potatoes with steak or lamb.) Keeping the heat fairly high, toss the mixture lightly until the wine has evaporated, about 2 or 3 minutes.

Serves 4 to 5.

Rut Etheridge made his first professional sale at the age of seven (a poem) to Look *magazine in 1956, certainly an auspicious literary beginning. For the past few decades he has written primarily on social issues for a wide range of prestigious newspapers, including the* Washington Post *and* Los Angeles Times. *His first published novel was* Legent of the Duelist *followed by the best-selling* The First Duelist. *He is currently working on a new trilogy.*

Rutledge E. Etheridge

¶D

Rut's Darn Good C'mon Try It Pasta/Tuna Salad

Two of my uncles fought in the Battle of the Bulge during World War II. They won. (They had help.) I've been fighting the battle since the age of nine, and it's still undecided. But I have help, too. This salad is virtually fat-free—and doesn't taste like it. My eternally slim wife and two likewise teenagers were big fans until they learned that it wasn't the "real" stuff that Dad's supposed to stay away from. Now it's, "No thanks, Pop, but it looks good, please pass the pork chops." Go figure.

Ingredients

First, shoot a tuna
Or: 1 (6½-ounce) can water-packed tuna, loosely drained and flaked
1 pound package vegetable rotini
⅓ cup sliced green salad olives
1½ teaspoons (roughly) Lawry's minced onion
1½ cups nonfat mayonnaise
½ teaspoon apple cider vinegar
1 teaspoon water (Perrier, if your guests are yuppies)
paprika

Directions

Cook rotini to desired texture. Combine remaining ingredients and stir vigorously. When you've reached your aerobic plateau, pour half of the mixture into a large salad bowl. Drain the cooked rotini and rinse thoroughly in cold water. Add to salad bowl and mix. Pour remaining goop on top, and mix again. Sprinkle with paprika, and cool, covered, for an hour or so.

Give it a try; surprise your friends and neighbors. Just don't tell the thin ones our little secret.

A baker's son from Rochester, New York, Eliot Fintushel is a solo theater performer and teacher. He was invited to succeed the abbot of Sonoma Mountain Zen Center, but wised up in time to save his soul and his good humor, and he began writing science fiction instead. He has since sold nearly two dozen stories to major science fiction magazines. He lives in California with his wife, New Yorker writer Noelle Oxenhandler, and their daughter, Ariel.

Eliot Fintushel

¶D

Bubby Sophie's Glass Tea

This is my grandmother Sophie Fintushel's recipe, passed down to me when I was seven.

Directions

1) Take it some water—the cold, the hot, I don't care from it. Into a tippot put it, big like your sister Mollie's head but only until she is three. Maybe better you should use it a saucepan; the hole is bigger. Don't make a mess, I'll gonna swing you around my head like a chicken.

2) Put op the fire—careful how you don't touch—and wait until it comes the *big* bobbles. The big bobbles I'm talking, not here a bobble, there a bobble.

3) In a gless put it a tibbeg, could be a Salada, could be a Lipton, I don't care from it.

4) Into the gless pour the water what you got bobbling on the fire. If you make a mess, as God is my witness, I'll gonna stuff horseradish in your *poopik*. Swish it a little bit the tibbeg. Take out and put it someplace you shouldn't get it dirty, you could always use it again, you know what I'm talking?

5) Between your teeth put it a sugar cube—a Domino is okay. Pick it op the gless tea, and through the sugar cube, trink. This is a fine gless tea what I told you, and this goes for your whole life.

Charles L. Fontenay was born in Brazil and reared on a farm in northwestern Tennessee. Several years after high school graduation, he began fifty years of newspaper work, interrupted only by service in World War II. He wrote science fiction regularly throughout the 1950s and early 1960s, publishing three novels and dozens of short stories and novelettes. After his retirement from the newspaper business, he took up science fiction again, producing a number of short works and starting a series of children's science fiction books. He adds, "I am a third degree black belt in Tae Kwon Do and have on occasion won awards for oil painting as well as for national correspondence chess play."

Charles L. Fontenay

ᵞᴰ

Chryse Coquillage

This is a dish I have often cooked for myself and sometimes for friends. It's one of the recipes I had in mind when I had some of my major characters eating dinner at the Hangwo Palace in the novel *Kipton and Gruff*. That's the reason for the name of the dish, as the Hangwo Palace is in The Pile, a module on the edge of the Chryse Planitia on Mars. Of course all food on Mars has to be imported from Earth (except for some vegetables grown in the Biobubble) and is very expensive.

I learned Chinese cooking when I was a young newspaperman in West Tennessee, from a Chinese friend who ran a laundry there, and cooked enough of it to become no longer dependent on recipes for my favorite dishes.

Ingredients

 2 tablespoons light soy sauce
 1 tablespoon rice wine or sherry
 1 teaspoon sugar
 4 slices fresh ginger
 8 ounces green shrimp, cleaned and deveined
 2 tablespoons olive or corn oil
 4 ounces fresh mushrooms, cleaned and sliced, mixed with 1 tablespoon
  light soy sauce
 1 large green pepper, cut into half-inch squares
 ½ red (sweet) pepper, cut into half-inch squares
 1 small can of sliced water chestnuts, drained
 1 tablespoon cornstarch

Directions

In a bowl mix a heaping tablespoon of cornstarch, 2 tablespoons of light soy sauce, 1 tablespoon of rice wine or sherry, 1 teaspoon of sugar, and 4 slices of fresh ginger. Mix in shrimp until thoroughly coated.

In a wok or large skillet heat two 2 tablespoons olive oil or corn oil very hot. Put in the mushrooms and stir for 1 minute, then put in the peppers and water chestnuts and stir for 2 minutes more. Take out.

Put in the flavored shrimp and stir for 3 minutes, then add ·the vegetables and stir together. Serve over steamed or fried rice.

Terry A. Garey is a fantasy writer and poet who has been published and has canned in many different places. She has written The Joy of Home Winemaking, *published this year. She adds, "In Vegetology my vegetable is pumpkin, with garlic as spice and soy sauce as condiment. Go figure."*

Terry A. Garey

ﹰﹰD

Spotting UFOs While Canning Tomatoes

(for Karen Schaffer, Laurie Winter, and Eleanor Arnason)

First, get your tomatoes
this is not always as easy as it seems
if you are going to go to all that trouble
they might as well be good ones:
      red, full of flavor, perfectly ripe
  not a lot of bruises
grow them yourself
or get them from a farmers' market:
      Big Boy, Big Girl, Roma, Royal Chico
  Super Beefsteak, Early Pick, Lady Luck, Rutgers,
I've canned them all
just be sure they're good

pick a cool evening to do this if you can
unfortunately
cool evenings and tomatoes rarely go together
think of your pioneer grandmothers
indian grandmothers
slave grandmothers
immigrant grandmothers,
putting up whole gardens for families of ten

and the hired hands
think of winter and canned tomatoes from the store
          tasting of tin
purse your lips in disgust
roll up your sleeves
and get to work
(a friend taught me to do this
long ago
when I was young and poor but had plenty of tomatoes
she put my tomato destiny in my own hands
as well as my peach, pear, applesauce and jelly destiny)

make sure you have enough jars, lids, rings and time
read through the instructions
(you know what your memory is like)
then fire up the canner and go for it

it's still the same hot water bath
taking too much room on the stove
a battered saucepan for scalding lids
bigger saucepan for scalding tomatoes
to make them easier to peel

then it's peel and core, my girl, peel and core
chop those tomatoes down
slip off the skins, keep the water hot

paring knife nicks, seeds spurt out
acids sting my skin
adds to the general redness

mere mortals should clear the kitchen
order out pizza—if they want to eat
it's like a marathon:

sweat, determination, endurance
going for the long distance—
you have to remember to drink water
so you don't dehydrate

as I go along, lift hot jars, dump water
push in the tomatoes, wipe the rims
leave a space for expansion
try to guess how much is enough
when I tighten down the lids
as I go along
        I philosophize
on the meaning of life
meditate on the smile of my grandmother
female bonding
female machisma
think about the farm women doing four times as much as this
every day all summer
and gasp, shake my head
I'll never understand how they did it

while the first batch boils I get ready for the next
try to stockpile against time and weariness
shift from one sore foot to another
wad up the newspapers, wipe up flooding juice
save skins for the compost

I glance out the kitchen window and spot moving lights in the sky
an airplane, I think,
then as the steam rises around my head I realize
there are no flight patterns out my kitchen window
my hands clench, I think : UFOs, Flying Saucers,
aliens, green monsters
tentacled sentient creatures who need women to:

can tomatoes?
The heck with them. Let them can their own tomatoes.

the kitchen's a mess
I've burned myself twice
used a bandaid
        scalded the inside of my arm with steam
but there are the first seven jars
and one by one
        ping!
  goes the beat of my heart as they seal down

take that, alien invaders

I work on into the night—not talking much—
hit a plateau
where it seems I'll never see the last bushel done
but finally
it's over
last jar is sealed
I dump the five gallons of hot water down the drain
so the canner won't rust
wipe down the counters
clean off the stove top
        touch once more all the women
everywhere, even outerspace aliens,
who put something aside for winter

Mark Garland is a young science fiction writer who makes his home in upstate New York. His wife, the cook of the family, provided the following favorite recipes.

Mark and Jenny Garland

ᵼᕲ

Absolute Chili
(Chili Con Carne)

Ingredients

1½ pounds ground beef or ground turkey
4 tablespoons onion
4 tablespoons diced green pepper
½ tablespoon minced garlic
4 tablespoons oil
2 cups tomato sauce
1 can tomato paste
1 teaspoon chili powder
½ teaspoon salt
1½ teaspoons sugar
1 no. 202 can (or 4 small cans) kidney beans with juice
4 already-cooked potatoes cut up

Directions

Sauté ground meat with onion, green pepper, and garlic. When cooked, add all other ingredients. Simmer for about 1 hour.

ᵼᕲ

Space Angel Delight

Ingredients

3 cups heavy cream
1 cup confectioners' sugar
1 teaspoon vanilla

2 cups milk
2 packages unflavored gelatin
1 cup cool water
1½ large or 2 small angel food cakes
any flavor fruit sauce you like (such as strawberry, raspberry, etc.)

Directions

Whip 3 cups heavy cream with electric beater. Add 1 cup confection-ers' sugar. Add vanilla. Slowly add milk.

Soak packages of unflavored gelatin in 1 cup cool water in a·small pan. Place small pan in larger pan of hot water over low heat until dissolved. Add gelatin to cream mixture. Break up angel food cake into two cake pans evenly. Pour well-mixed cream mixture over cake and pat down.

Chill about 3 hours. When serving, top with fruit sauce.

Meteor Meatloaf (a turkey of a loaf)

Ingredients

¾ of a medium-size onion
1 cup chopped celery
½ teaspoon salt
dash of pepper
2 slices of bread, broken up
¼ cup evaporated milk
1 egg
2 pounds meatloaf mix
1 pound ground turkey or beef

Directions

Mix all ingredients together and put in a buttered pan.
Bake at 350 degrees for 45 minutes to 1 hour.

David Gerrold's earliest successes were television scripts, most notable the "Trouble with Tribbles" episode of Star Trek, *which made him an instant cult favorite. He has since gone on to create the memorable AI novel* When H.A.R.L.I.E. Was One *and the* War Against the Cthorr *series. Currently he lives in California with his family.*

David Gerrold

ᵀ🍴

Salmon á là Gerrolde

This one is easy, so easy it's embarrassing.

Ingredients

    fresh salmon
    2 white onions
    2 beefsteak tomatoes
    lemon juice

Directions

You get yourself a healthy slab of fresh salmon, a couple white onions, and a couple beefsteak tomatoes. Slice the onions and tomatos and make a bed of the slices in a baking pan. Lay the salmon on top of it. Put another layer of onion and tomato slices on top. Squeeze fresh lemon juice all over everything—everything in the pan, that is. If you're lazy, you can use the bottled lemon juice. If you're feeling adventurous, sprinkle a little cooking sherry on this, and maybe even a little Italian dressing. Bake for 20 minutes at 325 degrees. Serve with fresh salad and white wine. (I prefer Coca-Cola myself.)

Some people like salmon, some don't. Salmon has a very strong flavor of its own that you can't really change; all you can do is dress it up a little according to your own tastes. Every time I make this, I try adding different flavors. It turns out fine every time.

Corned Beef and Cabbage

Most supermarkets sell corned beef in ready-to-go packages. You put it in a cauldron, bring it to a boil, and let it simmer for 2 or 3 hours. For most people, that's all there is to it. For best results, pick out a brisket that is fatty. (Yeah, I know. So what? Lean corned beef doesn't have enough flavor to justify the effort.)

But the real appeal of corned beef is the special flavor that the spices add to the meat. My trick is to add extra spices to the water. Some corned beef comes with extra spice packages. If not, you're on your own, and this will require some experimentation on your part to find the tastes you like; but it's worth the effort to do the research. If nothing else, I like to add a clove or two to the water to add a sweet overtone to the taste.

Where most people fail with corned beef and cabbage is in the cabbage. They boil it separately, and they let it sit in the pot until it turns into a gray mushy mess. *NO!!*

What you do is this: An hour before you serve, you put a couple of small onions in the water, several peeled potatoes (cut into quarters), and some scrubbed carrots. Let the veggies simmer with the beef. You want to cook the vegetables in the *same* water so that they pick up the sweet juicy flavors of the beef and the spices.

When the potatoes are cooked enough to eat, take the beef out and give it a minute to cool. Cut the cabbage into quarters and put it in the pot to cook in the same juices. Five to ten minutes is usually sufficient. The important thing is that the cabbage is best when it still has some of its crunch—*al dente*. Most people overcook. This is wrong. Cabbage has feelings too; it is not an add-on, it is integral to the meal.

Now slice the corned beef. By the time you're through slicing the corned beef, the cabbage will be just about ready. Scoop everything onto a big platter, serve with fresh bread and butter and a good strong beer. Suggested condiments are horseradish and mustard, but a well-prepared corned beef needs neither.

The best way to eat corned beef and cabbage is to spear a piece of cabbage, a piece of potato, and a piece of corned beef all on your fork at the same time, so that the flavors mix wonderfully in your mouth.

⫟◗

Spaghetti by Sean

This is one of my favorite dinners, and one of the easiest to prepare. My son Sean is the spaghetti chef in our house, and he's quite good at it, as several survivors will proudly attest.

Ingredients

    1 pound ground beef
    garlic to taste
    mushrooms to taste
    onions to taste
    tomato sauce
    1 can stewed sliced tomatoes
    salsa to taste
    spaghetti
    butter
    salt to taste

Directions

Brown some ground beef in a large frying pan. A pound is usually enough. Season to taste with garlic. Cut in mushrooms and onions. Let it simmer until everything is cooked. Now add your tomato sauce. I prefer Paul Newman's Industrial Strength Spaghetti sauce, but you may prefer something else. *Now add a can of stewed sliced tomatoes and some salsa to taste.* This kicks the flavor-level of this stuff up a couple of notches. While it simmers, make the spaghetti.

Here's the trick to making perfect pasta. Put butter and salt in the water before you add the noodles. Boil for no longer than eight minutes. As you approach the eight-minute mark, you want to test the noodles continually for just that right amount of biteness; what the Italians call *al dente.* After you drain the spaghetti, *rinse it in cold water.* This is to prevent it from getting gummy.

Some people like to mix the spaghetti and the sauce all together in the same bowl. I don't. I like to see a bed of naked white noodles, with a slather of sauce across the top. If you must add parmesan, get fresh not dried. Garlic bread is okay with this; I prefer sourdough myself.

![fork and knife symbol] 🍴

Death to the Enemies
of the Revolution Chili

Ingredients

2 good-size steaks
oil
garlic
2 pounds ground beef
beans
1 yellow onion
mushrooms
bell peppers
1 box cherry tomatoes
1 to 2 cans stewed sliced tomatoes
1 jar of Paul Newman's Industrial Strength Spaghetti Sauce
cheap red wine
1 can of shoestring-sliced beets
chocolate syrup
curry powder
cloves
red pepper
chili powder
optional: vegetables

Directions

Start with a couple of good-size steaks. I use top sirloin, but you can use a lesser grade if your guests don't deserve the best. Cut it into bite-size chunks. Brown the meat in oil, olive oil is best, and sprinkle liberally with garlic. Sear the chunks until they leap from the frying pan, screaming in pain. Put them in the cauldron. (What? You don't have a cauldron?)

Now, take a couple of pounds of ground beef—lean is good, fatty has more flavor—break it apart into little bits and brown the little bits in the oil too. Add them to the cauldron.

You may now add the beans. If you're lazy, you can use canned beans. (I'm lazy.) I usually use 1 can of kidney beans, but if I'm feeling extravagant, I'll add 2 or 3 different kinds of beans. Pinto beans are good too.

Take a fresh yellow onion, slice it, and chop the slices into reasonably small bits. Brown these in the used olive oil. Cut up some nice fat mushrooms and let these simmer in the same oil too. When the mushrooms are soft, add them to the cauldron. At this point, you may also slice in pieces of bell pepper. I prefer the red and yellow varieties because they're more sweet than bitter.

Now, it's time to start adding the tomatoes. Take a box of cherry tomatoes and cut each one in half, tossing the little buggers into the cauldron. Ignore their cries for help. (People who anthropomorphize their food shouldn't eat.) Add 1 or 2 cans of stewed sliced tomatoes and a jar of Paul Newman's Industrial Strength Spaghetti Sauce. Notice I'm not giving any sizes here—everything depends on the size of your cauldron. A certain amount of personal taste is demanded in any recipe, and remember, this is chili we're talking about.

All right, now we can start getting serious about flavor. First, get a bottle of cheap Dago red wine. If the wine costs more than $3, you spent too much. Pour two glasses. Pour one of the glasses into the chili, the other into yourself. Now, add a can of shoestring-sliced beets (yes!), some chocolate syrup (yes!), and enough curry powder to sting. Now add cloves and red pepper. Remember, this is cooking by ear. You're going to have to sample this every step of the way, or it will turn on you. If it gets sufficiently angry, you'll probably have to call in a Toxic Waste Disposal squad, so be careful. For safety's sake, I always try to balance stinging flavors with sweet ones; this creates a pleasantly deceptive taste that delivers a kick to the roof of the mouth that has to be experienced to be believed.

If you live in California, you may now add some veggies—okra, garbanzoes, a handful of bean sprouts, corn, whatever suits your fancy. This is where artistry is demanded. Season to taste with whatever kinds of peppers you like best. I like both red pepper and lemon pepper. Oh yes, and of course, you must add some chili powder. (Do not overdo it on the chili powder, as this will give the whole thing an unpleasant taste like chili.)

Simmer on low heat for an hour or two—if you can wait that long. This mess is just as good the second and third day; sometimes it gets even better after the ingredients have a chance to overcome their initial animosity at having been found in the same pot together. It also freezes remarkably well. My technique is to make a couple of cauldrons at a time and freeze most of it. But you'll need a sturdy freezer, one which will allow you to lock the chili inside until it behaves itself.

Serve this in big bowls, with thick slabs of fresh sourdough for mopping up. It's also good over rice or spaghetti. Top it off with a dollop of sour cream with a cherry tomato on top. Also add shredded cheddar, chopped olives, and chopped scallions. Red wine is appropriate, I prefer Coca-Cola.

This chili is so good the pan will lick itself clean. It's guaranteed to clear your sinuses, sandblast your tonsils, and keep your stomach churning for hours. It's the perfect cure for somnambulism, narcolepsy, and people with dropsy. Do not plan on sleeping for several days after you eat this stuff and have lots of those little chewable tablets around for people with weak constitutions.

The author assumes no responsibility. Make this stuff at your own risk. Lead gloves are recommended. Keep this stuff away from children and small animals.

Richard Gilliam's career includes more than twenty years of freelance nonfiction and several dozen well regarded short-stories. Many of his stories, including his Bram Stoker Award nominated "Caroline and Caleb," are drawn from the oral histories of his family. This recipe has been handed down from his grandmother, Mayme Gilliam (1900–1979), who routinely hosted twenty or more people each Sunday at her home.

Richard Gilliam

¶D

Asparagus Roll-Ups

Ingredients

    12 thin slices white bread
    8 slices bacon, cooked and crumbled
    8 ounces cream cheese
    12 cooked asparagus spears
    melted butter

Directions

Trim the crusts from the bread, then roll thin using a rolling pin. Blend the bacon with softened cream cheese and spread the mixture onto the bread slices. Lay a cold cooked asparagus spear on each bread slice and roll up. Place the roll-ups onto a baking sheet, making sure that the roll-ups are seam side down. Cover and refrigerate till serving time.

Just prior to serving, brush with melted butter, then broil until lightly browned. Serve hot.

James Gunn has written screenplays, radio scripts, articles, verse, and criticism, but most of his publications have been science fiction. He started writing SF in 1948, was a full-time freelance writer for four years, and has had 80 stories published in magazines and books. His novel The Immortals *was dramatized as an ABC-TV "Movie of the Week" and became an hour-long series,* The Immortal, *in 1970. Other novels include* The Listeners, The Joy Makers, *and* Star Bridge *(with Jack Williamson). He received a Hugo Award in 1983 for his nonfiction book,* Isaac Asimov: Foundations of Science Fiction, *and an Eaton Award for Lifetime Achievement in 1992.*

James Gunn

When I was growing up in Kansas City, Missouri, during the depression, lunch counters and hamburger joints were commonplace. Nowadays they have been driven out of business by the quick-food chains.

I was lucky: my father had a job as a printer all through the thirties. Still, we didn't eat out much. But stopping by a hamburger place wasn't really eating out: hamburgers may have cost 15 cents (those were the days when you could get a dozen White Castle hamburgers for a dollar). We had a favorite place; it was called Boydston's (for those familiar with Kansas City, it was on Independence Avenue next to the old Vista Theater), and, although it consisted of only a dozen stools at a counter and perhaps a couple of tables, it served the best hamburgers and chili in town. We discovered it because it was just around the corner from the building where we played duplicate bridge twice a week, and often we stopped there afterwards. Those were the days when we were innocent of heartburn and insomnia.

I learned to cook hamburgers from watching Boydston and his helper, and I have become the uncrowned hamburger maven of our family and immediate friends. I even make them occasionally for my students at the University of Kansas. The secret of Boydston's hamburgers was that they were cooked quickly on a grill—nothing but meat and strings of onion pressed into it—and the buns were warmed on top of the hamburgers while they were cooking. Hamburgers should be cooked only once on each side, long enough to cook the meat through so that no pink remains but not more than a few minutes on either side, because hamburgers cooked too long get rubbery and tough.

🍴

Boydston's Hamburgers

Ingredients

1 pound hamburger
1 onion (white or yellow), sliced extremely thin
1 package good-quality hamburger buns
1 dill pickle, sliced as thin as possible
salt and pepper
mustard
ketchup (if that's what you like)

Directions

Hamburger should be of good quality but not extra lean, since a bit of fat helps hold the patty together and most of the fat gets cooked out. Divide the hamburger into 4 to 6 patties (we prefer quarter-pounders). Boydston used to roll the hamburger into balls and flatten them onto his big, black grill with a heavy spatula, but that doesn't work too well with a skillet and most home spatulas aren't strong enough. Place patties in a heated skillet (no oil); put a good helping of sliced onions on top of each patty and mash them into the meat, flattening the hamburger in the process. Cook quickly at medium-high heat and when done on one side (no more than a few minutes), turn the onion side down and continue cooking. Place both halves of the buns on the patties to warm. When the other side is done, pick up the hamburger with the spatula and slide the patty between the halves of the buns. I prefer to top my hamburgers with a good helping of the thinly sliced pickles and French's prepared mustard, but others prefer ketchup or both. Baked beans, potato chips, or french fries go well, but the hamburger is simple fare and doesn't appreciate frills and fancy surroundings.

Boydston and his helper didn't offer much conversation with their food. In fact they refused to reveal the recipe for their chili. Maybe with good reason: If we had been able to duplicate it we might not have come back, even for the hamburgers. And Boydston's chili was exceptional: it was cooked separately from the beans, as all good chili is, but served over a layer of beans. Boydston's chili had little grease and no tomato flavor; perhaps it was prepared without tomato sauce. I remember the taste of it after 45 years; one evening, I recall, my parents brought me a helping at midnight in a cardboard container.

But Boydston's chili is lost to the ages. Fortunately, we were not dependent on Boydston's charity. My father had his own recipe that he discovered in Texas, where he was stationed in World War I before being sent with his tank corps to France. That Texas chili became so famous in Kansas City (he made big pots of it for parties and gatherings of all kinds, and served as many as 100 at a time) and in Lawrence, where we have made it for family and friends and for science-fiction acquaintances who drop by, that it has become known as:

🍴

Gunn Chili

Ingredients

1 pound hamburger
1 medium white or yellow onion, chopped or ground
1 clove garlic, minced or ground
1 chili pod (with seeds removed), minced or ground
1 teaspoon chili powder
1 (8-ounce) can of tomato sauce
1 tomato can of water
½ teaspoon dry mustard
½ teaspoon celery seed
1 (4-ounce) can of sliced mushrooms (or stems and pieces) (optional)
salt and pepper
8 ounces pinto beans

Directions

We usually make it in larger amounts; 5 or 6 pounds is average; it freezes well and is convenient to freeze in serving-size units. If we're going to feed a large number, we figure a half pound per person.

Cook the hamburger in a heavy pot until pink is gone. Add onion (frozen is handy) and garlic, chili pod (if you can't find the dark-red chili pods, add two extra teaspoons of chili powder), tomato sauce, water, dry mustard, celery seed, and mushrooms (you can drain them or simply add the mushroom juice in place of an equal amount of water). Add a bit of salt and pepper now. Simmer slowly. Cook for several hours. Even in smaller quantities, it should be cooked until the chili is thick and not soupy, "cooked down," my father would say. The longer the chili is cooked the better it is; it's also a good idea to prepare it the day before and leave it in the refrigerator overnight. This allows the spices to blend together and the chili to mellow (the fat also rises to the top and can be removed; here, too, tastes may vary: my father had been known to *add* grease). As the chili cooks, taste and add salt, pepper, and more chili powder, if desired. But be careful: the spices tend to grow more potent after the chili has rested.

Meanwhile—the other and final secret to good chili—cook the beans separately: not kidney beans, whose powerful flavor can overpower the best chili, but mild pinto beans, which turn pink when cooked. In a pinch, canned pinto heans are available, or even unadorned old-fashioned pork 'n' beans. Cover the bottom of a bowl with beans and then top with chili, both preferably drained of most liquid by the use of a perforated ladle. Serve with saltines, ketchup, dill pickle spears if desired, plenty of cold liquids (I prefer ice water, but beer is also good), and whatever else you like. Chili can also be served over spaghetti, when it is known as "spaghetti red," or macaroni, when some call it "chili-mac"; some like it without beans or anything else. I'm not enthusiastic about fancying up such a plebian dish with grated cheese or raw onion, since it may overpower the flavor; some people also have been known to add vinegar. I do like ketchup, however, and my wife thinks *that* overpowers the flavor.

A final word from my wife, whose editing of this recipe has eliminated many possible misunderstandings and who, if truth be told, has inherited the apron of chili maker in the family: This recipe tolerates a great deal of individual variations; chop the onions a little or a lot, add garlic or leave it out, put extra beans in the bowl or none, serve it soupy or dry; even add new ingredients, as the Gunns did with the mushrooms.

But (my final word) if you want true Gunn chili, follow the directions and try it before striking out on your own.

Joe Haldeman will always be remembered for his science fiction novels, particularly the Hugo and Nebula Award–winning The Forever War *(widely considered science fiction's answer to* Catch-22 *and one of the great antiwar novels of all time). His talents are not limited to science fiction, however—"Graves," a recent horror story, won a World Fantasy Award for best story of the year. Currently he lives in Florida with his wife, Gay.*

Joe Haldeman

The Thistle Divine

Herewith, a couple of recipes involving my favorite vegetable, the artichoke. When I was a little kid in the Territory of Alaska, in the late forties and early fifties, most of our vegetables had to be imported from the "lower 48," and the main cost was air freight, whether you wanted an avocado or a zucchini. My parents liked artichokes, and since they didn't cost that much more than cabbage, we had them all the time.

I never knew my mother to cook artichokes any other way than to boil the hell out of them and serve them with a dipping sauce of lemon butter. I was twenty before I encountered the exotic notion of serving the thistle cold, with mayonnaise. Ever since, I've been searching out recipes and experimenting.

Greek-style Artichokes

Ingredients

4 large artichokes, stripped and sliced an eighth of an inch thick, as below
2 lemons
olive oil
2 onions, coarsely chopped
4 to 8 cloves garlic, minced
4 potatoes, cooked and sliced a quarter-inch thick
1 sweet red pepper, cut in strips

Directions

To prepare the artichokes: Take a large bowl of cold water and add the juice of a lemon.

First, cut the stems off the artichokes and also the top third of the leaves, and discard; rub the cut parts with lemon juice so they don't discolor.

Second, pull off all of the large outer leaves (retaining the "meat" at the base as much as possible).

Third, working quickly with a heavy knife and a spoon—a grapefruit spoon works best—cut each artichoke in half lengthwise and spoon out the hairy "choke," then slice each half into eighth-inch increments lengthwise, throwing the slices into the cold lemon-water.

That's the hard part. Now take a heavy skillet and heat up a few tablespoons of olive oil, enough to make a thick coat, until the oil shimmers but doesn't smoke. Drain the artichoke slices in a colander, shake off extra water, and throw them in to sauté for a couple of minutes. Add the onions and garlic and sauté, stirring, for a couple more minutes. Now push it all to one side, add a little more oil, and cover the bottom of the frying pan with potatoes (heaping the artichokes, etc., on top). Let them sizzle for a few minutes, browning. Then turn the heat down low, mix everything up, add the pepper strips and juice of a lemon; then cover and let everything steam for a couple of minutes. Serve with oil and vinegar on the side.

(If I were cooking it just for myself, or for other people who like hot stuff, I'd add a generous shake of hot pepper flakes before the final steaming.)

Serves 4 as a vegetarian main course, 8 as a side dish.

🍴

"Cajun" Shrimp and Vegetable Boil

This one was adapted from a newspaper recipe—how could anything that has both shrimp and artichokes be other than irresistible?

Ingredients

6 quarts water
¼ cup pickling spice
4 tablespoons salt
2 teaspoons cayenne

4 each: small onions, peeled; large potatoes, halved; celery and carrots
    (peeled and cut in 4-inch chunks)
2 artichokes, trimmed, split down the middle
1 lemon, halved
3 whole garlic bulbs
2 pounds shrimp (unshelled)
a couple trays of ice cubes

Directions

Put the spice, salt, and cayenne in the water and boil for ten minutes. Then put in all the vegetables, lemon, and garlic. Cook just below the boil until the artichokes are tender, about 20 minutes. (If you have fresh corn, you might cut a couple of ears into quarters and throw them in at the 15-minute mark.)

Then add the shrimp and heat it to a fast boil. Now take it off the fire, throw in the ice cubes, and cover it. Let it sit for 15 minutes; drain, and serve. Make a dipping sauce for the shrimp with ketchup, Worcestershire, horseradish, lemon juice, and Louisiana hot sauce. Serve the vegetables with butter and lemon quarters.

Serves 4.

Charlene Harmon lives in Magna, Utah, with her husband and three children. She graduated from BYU with a B.A. in English and Spanish (and a minor in history). While in college she was president of the science fiction and fantasy club and an editor on a semi-prozine called The Leading Edge. *Her publications include poems in magazines like* Amazing Stories, Sunstone, *and* Midnight Zoo, *and short fiction in anthologies.*

Charlene C. Harmon

¶⫇

Beef Casserole Augussa á là Al Carlisle (my father)

Ingredients:

- 1 pound hamburger
- ¼ to ½ cup onion, chopped
- 1 cup celery
- 1 package frozen peas
- ½ can bean sprouts
- ¼ cup milk
- 1 can cream of mushroom soup

Directions

Brown hamburger with onion. Add celery, peas, and bean sprouts. Then add the milk and soup. Bake for about 1 hour at 350 degrees. Cover with grated cheese, potato chips, or crackers if you wish. Serves 6.

Can also be cooked on the stove in a skillet for 20 to 30 minutes.

¶⫇

Baked Herb Chicken

Ingredients

4 or 6 chicken breasts, frozen. (You can add as many as you wish. I like using frozen chicken breasts because I buy in bulk and keep them in

the freezer. Fresh chicken can be substituted, but adjust the cooking time.)

sage (fresh or dried)
lemon herb seasoning
Italian seasoning
salt
1 can cream of chicken or cream of mushroom soup

Directions

Place chicken breasts in a large pan. (Any pan will do as long as it has sides. I use an 8 x 8-inch or a 9 x 13-inch pan.) Sprinkle both sides of chicken with sage, lemon herb seasoning, Italian seasoning, and a dash of salt, then drop the soup by spoonfuls onto the chicken. Cover the pan with aluminum foil. Bake at 350 degrees for 1 hour.

Can be served over rice. You can also cover the mixture with dry stuffing mix before baking.

Catalina Chicken á là JoAnn Carlisle (my mother)

Directions

Place whole chicken in a crock pot. Add a bottle of Catalina French dressing. Cook on low for 3 hours or until chicken falls off the bone.
Serve over rice.

Chocolate Chip Cookies

Ingredients:

$2/3$ cup soft shortening, part butter
$1/3$ cup granulated sugar
$1/2$ cup brown sugar, packed
1 egg
1 teaspoon vanilla

1½ cups sifted flour
½ teaspoon baking soda
½ teaspoon salt
1 cup Quaker Oats
½ cup walnuts, chopped
6 ounces semisweet, dark, and white chocolate chips. (Mint and peanut butter chips can be used, too, but they change the flavor of the cookies.)
¼ to ½ cup caramel pieces, cut up into tiny pieces
¼ to ½ cup marshmallows, cut into tiny pieces
¼ to ½ cup shredded coconut

Directions

Mix thoroughly: shortening/butter, granulated sugar, brown sugar, egg, and vanilla. Sift together and stir in flour, baking soda, salt. Stir in Quaker Oats. Then add walnuts, semisweet, dark, and white chips (or mint and peanut butter chips), caramel pieces, marshmallows, and coconut. Drop by teaspoon onto a cookie sheet. Bake at 375 degrees for 8 to 10 minutes.

Dill Pickles

Ingredients for vinegar mixture

5 quarts water
1 quart white vinegar
1 cup table salt (not iodized)

Ingredients for pickles (quantity varies; depends on the number of jars you want to bottle)

Concord grape leaves
garlic cloves
sprigs of dill
cucumbers (washed and dried)
red chili peppers

You will also need

Sterilized Kerr bottles with seals and lids

Directions

Combine ingredients for vinegar mixture and bring to a boil.

Put seals in a pan of water and bring to a boil. Set aside, but make sure the seals are still hot.

Place 1 Concord grape leaf in the bottom of a sterilized bottle. Add 1 clove of garlic (optional), then 3 to 6 sprigs of dill (depending on size of sprigs). Fill the bottle with cucumbers. Be careful not to overfill (so you can still seal the bottle). Pour vinegar mixture over top, covering all the cucumbers. Place another Concord grape leaf and 1 red chili pepper on top.

Put seal and lid on bottle. Set aside to cool. Lid will seal as it cools. If it doesn't seal, reheat.

It takes a few weeks for pickles to be ready. They can be stored for several years.

Marilyn J. Holt makes her home in Washington State. Her work includes both fiction and nonfiction, and she is a member of Science Fiction Writers of America as well as the Mystery Writers of America. As might be guessed from the reminiscence below, she cofounded and codirected the Clarion West Writers' Workshop. When not writing fiction, she writes about entrepreneurial business. She is a mergers and acquisitions specialist with one of the nation's premiere business brokerage firms.

Marilyn J. Holt

The first year (1984!) of Clarion West was tough on both the codirectors, J. T. Stewart and me. By the sixth week I could have taken Vonda McIntyre up on her offer to find us a good shrink (an offer she make when we announced that we were starting Clarion West, a decade after Vonda had given it up). The sixth week was taught by Norman Spinrad. He had the exhausted group each write a book proposal.

By the end of Clarion, everyone is tired, poor, and hungry (including the directors), so we decided to go to a Moroccan restaurant called Mammounia, near the Clarion West site. It is one of the few four star restaurants in Seattle.

Because of the number of people, we had a meza (feast), for which one pays a fixed amount for a nine or ten course meal. The only thing we could choose was the wine. Norman went into ecstasy about the quality and price of the Moroccan wine. He guided us through what could have been an overwhelming eating experience and ensured that we drank the most complementary wine with each course. He also made sure that those of us who were so tired that we could fall asleep even in the presence of fine food, stayed awake, eating, drinking, and making merry.

Several million people who are not SF fans know Norman as a restaurant reviewer in LA. Throughout the evening, he regaled us with stories about being a restaurant reviewer, wonderful food, how Moroccan wine is bottled (our bottles were hand made). He acted as the conductor of a symphony of fine food. Norman's a wonderful writing teacher, too. Many of the Clarion West graduates he taught became published authors.

As I write this, May 1995, Clarion West is poised to begin its twelfth year.

¶D

Marian Walker Carl's Crisp Dill Pickles

Marian Carl was my aunt on my mother's side. She would have liked SF fandom, had she known it existed. If there was another person in the area, she had a party. She would have been the queen of room parties. She and her older sister Helen (who entertained more sedately, and did read SF) were fabulous cooks. They both improvised and invented. I found this recipe in Helen's recipe file.

Ingredients

Cucumbers—select the size you like for pickles. Pick enough to fill 8 quart jars.
ground black pepper (1 pinch per jar, or to taste)
garlic cloves, slivered (2 cloves to jar, or to taste)
16 heads of dill (2 heads for each jar)
1 quart of vinegar—white apple vinegar is what my aunts used, but use the type you like—however, do not use red vinegar
3 quarts water
⅞ cup (14 tablespoons) finely granulated salt
½ teaspoon alum

Directions

Wash cucumbers, leave whole with about an eighth of an inch of stem. Soak in iced water overnight, then discard water.

In clean* quart jars (wide mouth jars are easiest to fill), pack cucumbers in tightly. Add pepper, slivered garlic, and dill heads to each jar.

In a saucepan, combine vinegar, water, salt, and alum. Bring to a boil. Pour boiling liquid over the cucumbers and seal jars immediately.**

Allow to ferment at least 2 weeks. Sealed, these will keep for years. If jars do not seal, or you do not want to seal them, store the jars in the refrigerator after allowing them to ferment for about 2 weeks.

Makes 8 quarts of pickles.

---

*Clean means washed, then scaled in boiling water for a minimum of 2 minutes.

**This recipe uses the hot pack method, so boil the lids for at least 1 minute, then put them on the jars and seal with the rings. Screw down the rings as tightly as you can. Jars, lids, and rings can be bought at most grocery stores.

Ⓨ🅳

Chili Rellenos Zero-Gravity Quiche

This is my recipe. I love chili rellenos, but they are a mess to make, and do not travel or store well. I also love quiche. So I mixed the two together. Because the crust is so easy, this is one quiche that you can actually make for dinner after a day in cyberspace. Serve with fresh fruit and sweet rolls or tortillas. It also adds a bit of spice to a brunch.

Ingredients for crust

 1¼ cups (Masa Harina Instant) masa mix or finely ground cornmeal of any color. I like blue cornmeal for this.
 ²/3 cup cold water
 2 tablespoons vegetable oil
 ¾ teaspoon salt

Directions for crust

 Combine ingredients in a 9-inch pie plate. Press to bottom and sides of plate to form crust.

Ingredients for filling

 5 eggs (5 egg whites, 2 yolks, and 3 tablespoons water work well too)
 1 (7-ounce) can sweet green chilies, diced
 ½ fresh jalapeño pepper, finely diced (if canned use 1 tablespoon diced [or to taste])
 8 ounces jack cheese or cheddar cheese

Directions for filling

 Separate eggs, beat whites until firm. Fold in yolks. Fold in chilies and cheese. Pour into pie plate.
 Bake at 375 degrees for 30 minutes. Test if done with a knife as you would a soufflé. If the knife comes out clean, it's done. Let pie cool for 5 minutes and serve.

C. Bruce Hunter is a journalist and educator whose work ranges from specialty dictionaries and college entrance tests to fantasy role playing materials. He is the author of four nonfiction books and more than ninety articles and short stories. His fiction has appeared in many of the science fiction magazines. A recent book, Beneath the Stone, details the history of masonic secrecy through thirteen centuries. He is currently writing a series of novels about magic and secrecy in the ancient world.

C. Bruce Hunter

🍴

Mandarin Flambé
(A Dessert)

This recipe is an example of an accidental discovery that turned out well. One morning several years ago, I concocted it from ingredients I found in a girlfriend's kitchen. The first time around, it was a quick breakfast dictated by necessity—there were no "traditional" breakfast foods in the house that morning. But the sauce is really too rich for early morning consumption, and it quickly evolved into a romantic dessert with ice cream. Try it on a special occasion, after supper for two, with candle light and soft music.

Ingredients

2 to 3 tablespoons butter or margarine
3 tablespoons brown sugar
1 (8-ounce) can pineapple chunks, well drained
12 maraschino cherries
1 to 2 ounces almonds or pecans, chopped (optional)
1 tablespoon lemon curd or zest of ½ lemon
1 (11-ounce) can mandarin orange segments, well drained
1 to 2 ounces 151 proof rum, warmed
premium vanilla ice cream

Directions

Melt butter over medium heat in a sauté pan. Add brown sugar and stir until melted. Add pineapple, cherries, and nuts to taste and heat through. Add lemon curd or zest and orange segments. Stir until sauce is smooth. At the table, flame with rum. Serve warm over ice cream. (Low-fat ice cream or frozen yogurt may be substituted.) Serves 6.

Dean Ing has been a USAF crew chief, senior research engineer and rocket designer, university professor, and a builder/driver of sports-racing cars. His published works are peppered throughout libraries: thrillers, mysteries, science fiction, and nonfiction. They range from a short scholarly text on failure analysis through articles on civil defense and backpacker equipment to a New York Times best-selling techno-thriller. Ing also develops and flies models of his fictional aircraft; develops aerodynamic devices to improve vehicle mileage; fly fishes; and raises indoor food plants. He has four grown daughters. With his wife, Gina, he lives in Oregon.

Dean Ing

Metaphor

When a book of mine is accepted, I sometimes toss a Bookends' party—the book, after all, *ends*. One night with thirty folks on the mountain with me, we got a black-ice snap. Plenty of gin and vermouth but olives didn't last. But there were shoals of pimientos and olive brine, so we simply made martinis with pimientos instead of olives. We dubbed it a "Metaphor." It is, after all, a metaphor of a martini; and in the future you can ask the bartender to mix you a metaphor. Works for me . . .

Ingredients

2 jiggers gin, chilled in freezer
$^1/_3$ jigger white vermouth
few drops ordinary sherry
a few pimiento pieces in brine

Directions

Combine and stir

Note: Perhaps I should specify that the martini buffs at my home *couldn't* get down the hill. Correction: they could, but couldn't get back up. That's why they tried the "Metaphor," and after a couple of jolts they got so tickled about "mixing metaphors" they forgot to complain.

⅌🍴

Sopa Anasazi

En route to writing *Anasazi* for *Analog*'s editor Stan Schmidt, I learned what Anasazi had to make stew, and in the novel I refer to it as Sopa Anasazi. Stan said he knew damn well I'd tried it (I had) and demanded the recipe. In fact, as I recall, I served it to him when he visited later.

Ingredients

2 cups squash, yellow or Zucchini, bite-size
2 cups stewed tomatoes (small or cut bite-size)
1½ cups shredded cooked turkey, dark meat
1 to 1½ cups corn kernels
2 teaspoons sea salt
small red peppers to suit, finely diced (don't get too frisky here; too much
    heat can ruin you)
1 teaspoon fresh ground sage

Directions

Toss it in stewpot and simmer till squash is done. Serves 4.

Anasazi kept turkeys and short-face dogs as pets and food, so you could try tender Bowsermeat if you crave authenticity. Capt. Wm. Clark's absolute favorite food was puppy stew. No wonder Lewis and Clark had to go live with the redskins!

Damon Knight is one of the grand old men of science fiction. A member of the Futurians—the group that included such other masters as Isaac Asimov, Frederik Pohl, Donald Wollheim, and many others who would revolutionize the field—he has gone on to produce such classics as Why Do Birds, The World and Thorinn, and CV. He currently lives in Oregon with his wife and fellow writer, Kate Wilhelm.

Damon Knight

❦

Onion-Apple Pork Stew

This is a hearty dish; the apple, onion, and cinnamon complement the pork in a very pleasant way.

Ingredients

boneless pork, cubed
butter
oil
1 big onion, chopped fine
2 garlic cloves, minced
1 slice of bacon, minced
apple juice or cider
salt
pepper
cinnamon
rosemary
lemon juice
cornstarch
water

Directions

Cut boneless pork into cubes and sauté in butter and oil until brown. Add a big onion, chopped fine, a couple of minced garlic cloves, and a slice of bacon, also minced; sauté some more until the onion is soft. Add apple juice or cider to half cover the meat. Season with salt, pepper, cinnamon, and rosemary. Simmer for 1½ hours or until tender. Taste for seasoning; add lemon juice if needed. Thicken sauce with a paste of cornstarch and water and serve hot.

Katherine Kurtz is the author of numerous best-selling fantasy novels, including the classic Chronicles of the Deryni series, which includes the trilogies The Legends of Camber of Culdi, The Heirs of St. Camber, and The Histories of King Kelsen. Her other works include Lammas Night and (with Deborah Turner Harris) The Adept.

Katherine Kurtz

🍴

Tuna Lasagna

I know: tuna lasagna sounds—well, blech! But it's easy, inexpensive, and seems to evaporate whenever I take it anywhere. The marinara sauce does something to the tuna, so that it tastes more like chicken.

Ingredients

6 lasagna noodles (⅓ package)
1 pound creamed cottage cheese
1 egg
½ teaspoon salt
dash pepper
1 cup grated Romano/Parmesan cheese
2 cans (10¼ ounces each) marinara sauce (2½ cups)
2 cans (7 ounces each) tuna, drained (water-packed is best)
½ teaspoon oregano
1 package (6 ounces) slice mozzarella cheese

Directions

Cook, rinse, and drain the lasagna noodles. Combine cottage cheese, egg, salt, pepper, and ¾ cup grated cheese. Spoon ⅓ cup marinara sauce in bottom of buttered 12 x 7½ x 2-inch baking dish; place 3 cooked lasagna noodles lengthwise in dish. Cover with cottage cheese mixture. Spread tuna over cottage cheese (or you can mix the tuna with the cottage cheese and then spread the lot over the noodles). Cover with remaining noodles. Spread with the remaining marinara sauce. Sprinkle with ¼ cup grated cheese and ½ teaspoon oregano. Cover with sliced mozzarella cheese. Cover dish with foil and bake 20 minutes at 350 degrees. Remove foil and bake 10 more minutes. Serve with hot garlic bread and a tossed green salad. Serves 6.

¶❸

Spice Cake

This is a fast, easy, and incredibly tasty recipe that I thought was also goofproof—until Anne McCaffrey tried it, using Irish baking soda, and we discovered that Sommerville and Ross of "Irish R.M." fame were right. Concerning soda, as well as just about everything else, "Things are different in Ireland."

Barring soda disasters, however, the recipe really is just about foolproof. (You'll also dirty a minimum of dishes putting it together.) In addition, the finished product stays moist and tasty for days (if it lasts that long) and freezes very well. The original recipe goes back at least three generations in my family and has Pennsylvania Dutch roots. The cardamom was my particular addition to the canon.

Ingredients

2 cups water
1 cup raisins
1¾ cups flour
1 cup sugar
½ teaspoon salt
1 teaspoon baking soda (American)
1 teaspoon each: cinnamon, ground cloves, and nutmeg (also ground cardamom, if you can find it)
½ cup butter
1 teaspoon vanilla
1 egg, well beaten
½ cup chopped nuts (optional)

Directions

Use about a 2-quart saucepan to boil the raisins in the water for about 10 minutes. I prefer golden raisins to the usual sort, but the end result of boiling is that either kind gets plump and tender. While the raisins are boiling, combine all the dry ingredients in another container. Add the butter to the hot raisin mixture and let it cool. Add the vanilla. Stir the dry ingredients into the raisin mixture—that's right, in the saucepan. Blend in well-beaten egg. Stir in nuts, if desired.

Pour into a 10 x 14 x 2-inch pan, greased and floured, or 24 paper muffin cups (supported in muffin tins).

Bake at 350 degrees for 40 minutes (less for cupcakes).

When cool, frost with buttercream frosting (recipe below).

As cupcakes, these are excellent picnic fare. You can even omit the frosting, since the cake itself is so rich and moist. They also make marvelous individual tea cakes—but do peel off the papers before frosting, so your guests don't have to manhandle them and then wonder what to do with the sticky papers, not to mention their sticky fingers.

ᵞⅅ

Buttercream Frosting

Ingredients

½ cup butter or margerine, softened
1 teaspoon vanilla
1 package confectioners' sugar
1 to 2 tablespoons milk

Directions

Cream softened butter with vanilla and begin slowly blending in sugar. Continue adding sugar, also adding milk from time to time, until you have enough frosting. You may need to add a bit more milk to keep frosting at proper spreading consistency.

ᵞⅅ

Katherine Kurtz's Drop Scones

"Proper" scones, however, are supposed to be rolled out and cut with a cookie-cutter, then baked on a traditional cast-iron "gridle." This is too time-consuming for my busy schedule—but I do love scones. So I finally searched out and refined a recipe for "drop" scones, that taste about the same but don't require rolling or cutting. These are quick and easy enough to whip up at a moment's notice, and will earn rave reviews when and wherever presented. If you premeasure the dry ingredients ahead of time, you can stir in the milk and egg when your guests arrive and have your scones in and out of the oven by the time the kettle has boiled and tea has brewed.

Ingredients

> 2 cups flour
> 2 heaping teaspoons baking powder
> 3 tablespoons sugar
> ¼ teaspoon salt
> dash of cinnamon
> 1 egg
> 1 cup milk

Directions

Stir together dry ingredients. Beat egg and milk together and pour into flour. Mix very thoroughly until creamy. Drop small spoonfuls in 12 well-greased muffin cups. (Do *not* use muffin papers, they stick!) You should get a dozen, depending on size. Bake 10 to 15 minutes at 450 degrees (200° C) until well risen and lightly browned.

Serve hot, with butter and strawberry jam—and Devonshire clotted cream, if you can get it!

Mercedes (Misty) Lackey has rapidly risen to the fore among the current crop of fantasy writers, producing many memorable novels, including the Last Herald-Mage series, the Heralds of Valdemar trilogy, the Vows and Honor novels, the Diana Tregarde Investigations, and many others. Among her most frequent collaborators is Larry Dixon, and together they have written nearly a dozen novels. Ms. Lackey has also written novels with such notables as Anne McCaffrey, Andre Norton, Marion Zimmer Bradley, and Piers Anthony.

Mercedes Lackey and Larry Dixon

🍴

We don't cook much. In fact, as anyone searching out freezer would discover, there is more space devoted to food for our rehab raptors than to us. Hence, the following recipes.

🍴

Food

by Mercedes Lackey

1. Go to freezer.
2. Make selection.
3. Verify that selection is not a frozen rat or mouse.
4. Go to microwave.
5. Put food in microwave.
6. Set microwave.
7. Remove food from microwave.
8. Eat.

Food 2

by Larry Dixon

1. Announce hunger.
2. Go to car.
3. Drive to fast-food restaurant.
4. Make selection.
5. Eat.

Alice Laurence works in the public relations department of a major corporation. "Most recent accomplishment: Won an International Association of Business Communicators Gold Quill (the Oscar of PR) for a speech written as a 'Shakespearean' (well. . . .) poem. A friend showed this masterpiece to a young man reluctantly studying Shakespeare in college and he told her: 'I think Shakespeare is better—only a bit, perhaps, but at least a bit.' Now I know what I want on my tombstone." Her science fiction has appeared in quite a few magazines and anthologies.

Alice Laurence

🍴

Salmon á là Cholesterol

I have discovered an appalling taste in myself of late: I actually prefer leftovers to the meal itself. It started with preferring the Friday after to Thanksgiving, and has progressed to the point where it dictates a good part of my meal planning, if one can call what I do "planning." What I call planning actually more closely resembles a juggler on the kind of medicine that gives you the shakes. What I'm usually juggling is budget ("You don't get paid till *next* week?"), time ("If I make spaghetti, we won't eat till ten!"), and finding a substitute for some crucial ingredient I forgot in the supermarket ("There must be something you can use in place of onions!").

But I digress. I like leftovers and I've collected recipes that use them and, when pushed to the wall, invented a few to avoid tossing something I'm sure will taste better the second day. This is one of those inventions.

Directions

1. Start by having salmon for dinner the night before. Buy enough so you'll have 1½ to 2 steaks (or filets) left.

2. Cook a package of noodles the minimum time (taste one to make sure it isn't still hard). While they're cooking, break up the leftover salmon into small pieces.

3. Drain the noodles and leave them in the colander while you.

4. Melt about ²/₃ cup of butter in a large skillet. You could probably use margarine or olive oil, but my doctor doesn't call me the "Cholesterol Poster Child" for nothing.

5. As soon as it's melted, dump the noodles in and toss them around, then add about a third of a cup of grated Parmesan cheese, and toss some more.

6. Add a large can or jar of drained mushrooms and a large can of LeSeur peas (also drained)—you could use any green vegetable you like; I like peas and the color is just right—and toss again.

7. Add the crumbled salmon (I suppose you could use canned salmon, but I never have; you could probably use other kinds of fish or even chicken, but the color of the salmon against the yellow noodles with the green peas makes it appealing to the eye) and toss again. Keep tossing (the cheese makes it stick if you don't) until it's hot enough to serve. You'll get about four servings. If you're the only one eating it, freeze the other three servings. They reheat in the microwave quite tolerably (add a pat or two of butter when you put it in the microwave).

8. Eat cautiously; no matter how careful you are, you'll miss at least one bone.

General wisdom has it that men don't like to cook. They prefer to barbecue. Pooh-pah from Lucas K. Law, a petroleum engineer and a published author of articles and short stories, in Calgary, Canada. He doesn't believe it; most men (especially writers) just want something easy and quick and "Soya Sauce Stewed Chicken" is a recipe from his mother's treasure chest. It is a clear favourite with his family members on any occasion. Lucas wishes to thank his mother, Florence, a restaurant consultant, for continuing to share her cooking expertise.

Lucas Law

❦

Soya Sauce Stewed Chicken (Triple-S Chicken)

Ingredients

> 1 (2-pound) chicken
> 1 tablespoon sesame oil
> 10 slices ginger
> 2 cloves garlic, chopped fine
> ½ teaspoon salt
> ½ teaspoon sugar
> 5 tablespoons soya sauce
> 2 tablespoons oyster sauce
> 2 tablespoons cooking wine
> dash of pepper
> 2 cups water
> *Optional:* Mix the following until smooth:
> > 1 tablespoon corn flour
> > ½ cup water

Directions

Cut chicken into bite-size pieces.

Heat sesame oil in pan. Fry ginger and garlic. Put in chicken and fry for 3 to 4 minutes.

Add salt, sugar, soya sauce, oyster sauce, cooking wine, pepper, and water. Note: Vegetables (e.g., carrot, onions, turnip, mushrooms) can be added.

Simmer for 15 to 20 minutes until cooked.

Thicken with corn flour mixture.
Serve hot with rice, pasta, potatoes, or bread.

Family secret: The leftovers usually taste better the next day; just warm them up in the microwave.

A twenty-year resident of Alaska, Hugh says he owes the pierogi recipe to a "fortuitous marriage to a beautiful Polish Princess" named Susan. Both were students living out of their backpacks when they first met. With their youngest child nearly an adult, it may be time to dust off the backpacks and roll down the road again.

But this time they will do it in a camper.

Hugh Leddy

ᵓᴰ

Polish Pierogi á là Pluto

Since Poles at one time or another have ranked among the top leaders in the advance of scientific thought—(Copernicus and Ma'm'selle Marie Curie being among the most noted)—it seems only fitting that a traditional Polish treat be included in *Serve It Forth!*

Herewith is offered my wife's family recipe for pierogi.

Ingredients

1 pint sour cream
4 eggs
1 tablespoon salt
4 cups flour
Filling materials (Please note: the fillings can be adapted to include cheeses or other ingredients, even fruit jellies, whatever you desire. Be original, and it will be more fun!)

Directions

Mix sour cream, eggs, and salt together. To this take 4 cups flour (or more if desired)—add all at once and mix well. Let sit 1 hour with a towel over the bowl. Roll out about an eighth- to a quarter-inch thick. (Take only ⅓ of the total amount of dough at a time to roll out. Keep all the scraps from previous rollings to use in the final rolling and use only enough flour to make sure the dough doesn't stick.) Cut into 3-inch or 3½-inch rounds. Place a measuring spoon/tablespoon heap of cheese mixture on ½ the round near the center and fold over and press edges together. You should now have a half-moon shape.

Place in a large kettle of salted, boiling water—leave plenty of room between each pierogi so they don't stick together. They will fall to the bottom of the kettle and then pop to the top when done. This will be a matter of a few minutes. Water should not be allowed to boil too hard.

Remove from water with a slotted spoon and let drain. They are now ready to fry until golden brown on both sides in butter or margarine—or they can be eaten just as they are.

Good with a dab of sour cream and, of course, Kielbasa (Polish sausage) fried!

Bardzo Smaczne!!!!

(Very tasty!!!!)

Tom Ligon has degrees in Biology and Engineering Technology and has spent most of the last twenty years working for a number of technology companies in Northern Virginia. Recently he formed his own consulting service, Assorted Technical Expertise. Clients include a physicist well known in SF circles, who would rather keep a low profile for the moment, and Aerodesic Research, an outfit building a manned single-stage-to-orbit rocket in a barn. As one might expect from his background, his short fiction (including a number of cover stories) can frequently be found in Analog Science Fiction and Fact. *He adds, "Generally my stories involve 'hard science,' but I try to remember that stories are about people." He lists his other interests as flying, computers, photography, carpentry, hiking, and outdoor activities.*

Tom Ligon

‖D

Experimental Therapeutic Bread

Breadmaking, the old-fashioned way, can be great therapy. There are *thousands* of easier recipes. This one is good exercise, a great way to vent frustration, and has been known to overcome writer's block. However, it requires no great skill or magic, and anyone can do it. The process is delightfully messy and creative, and remarkably noncritical in many ways. Part of the fun is the experimental aspect: play with the ingredients and methods with confidence. Most probably, no two batches will turn out exactly alike, but most efforts will reward you with a hearty, tasty, old-fashioned bread you will eat for its own sake, not as an edible napkin to keep the peanut butter off your fingers. This is *not* a good recipe for a bread-making machine, as it will probably stick. Lots of calories, but you will *earn* them. Besides, you are unlikely to make this often enough to be a large part of your diet.

Ingredients (today, anyway)

    2 packs yeast (active dry is OK)
    ½ cup warm water
    2 cups skim milk (adjust for desired dough texture)
    2 tablespoons margarine
    ¼ cup honey
    4 egg whites (cholesterol, yuh know)
    3 cups whole wheat flour
    3 cups unbleached white flour
    ½ cup cornmeal

Substitutions and Modifications

High-gluten flour for unbleached white (for French bread texture)
Adjust proportions of flour
Substitute oil or butter for margarine
2 eggs for 4 egg whites (starving young writers *need* cholesterol)
Sugar or molasses for honey
Water or whole milk for skim
Beer for *part* of the fluids above
Add sunflower seeds, nuts, dried fruit, etc.
Add sourdough starter

Directions

Mix the yeast per package instructions, typically in ½ cup lukewarm water with a couple of teaspoons of honey or sugar. Let the yeast stand until it is foaming to beat the band (and if it doesn't, get fresh yeast). The mixing below is best done in a large mixing bowl, about 3 quarts capacity. Warm ½ cup of the milk slightly in a microwave or oven (105 degrees is ideal). Melt the margarine using gentle heat. Add the honey, margarine, eggs, and yeast to the milk and mix well. Begin adding flour while mixing until the mixture becomes too thick to stir.

Now the fun and mess begin. Rub a little margarine on your hands, then sprinkle them with flour to reduce sticking. Continue adding the remainder of the flour while kneading the dough to mix thoroughly. When the dough becomes tough enough to hold up with one hand, transfer to a clean counter or bread-making pad that has been sprinkled with flour. If the dough appears too dry, add a bit more liquid. The dough should be tough and stretchy. Keep a little dry flour on the kneading surface and your hands to help prevent sticking.

Put the dough back in the mixing bowl and cover with aluminum foil. Allow the dough to stand in a warm place and rise until it has at least doubled, preferably tripled in volume. I usually preheat the oven slightly, then turn it off and put the bowl in. If the dough fails to rise within about 3 hours, the yeast is either dead or you did something it disliked, like getting it too hot or giving it enough beer to put it to sleep. Mix some more yeast and knead it *thoroughly* into the dough. Never microwave the yeast—nuking seems to kill it.

Uncover the dough, punch it down, powder it with flour. and knead it again. Stretch it, flatten it, roll it up, ball it up, fold it over, and otherwise feed air to the little yeast cells so they make carbon dioxide efficiently and make the bread rise. Knead it until all your aggravations are gone, and preferably until you have a well-formed story idea. If this isn't a workout, you aren't doing it right. You can allow it to rise again and knead as before, or go ahead and form it into loaves now.

I make 2 or 3 loaves, either hand-formed or in bread pans, and you can also make hamburger buns, etc. Just before forming the loaves, I massage the dough thoroughly to eliminate all the seams produced by kneading. I coat the inside of the bread pans with a thin coat of margarine, and sprinkle fresh flour over the dough before placing in bread pans. You can also brush a little melted margarine over the top for a softer crust. Allow the dough to rise again to about the volume you want, then gently put it into a 350-degree oven (more or less—experiment!) and bake, oh, maybe 45 minutes to an hour, until the crust is golden-brown and the smell makes you crazy. While it is baking, clean up the mess, or your better half will have your hide.

My tradition is to cut a slice, or two, or three, while the bread is still hot. Butter and honey are the only spreads for a purist at this point. If the bread is any good, this is a good time to call over the neighbors. If it didn't work out so well, cut it up for croutons and try again some time. Generally, if the yeast is good and you get a suitable dough texture, some good will come of it. Impatience and bad yeast are the most likely causes of failure, though I suspect you could come up with substitute ingredients that produce something wretched if you tried hard enough.

🍴

Divinity
by Linda Ligon (Tom's Lovely Wife)

Ingredients

    2 cups regular sugar
    ½ cup clear Karo syrup
    ½ cup water
    2 egg whites
    1 teaspoon vanilla
    1 cup nuts, chopped

Directions

Mix sugar, syrup, and water well in pan; cook to hard boil stage of candy thermometer on medium-high heat. Stir while cooking. Beat egg whites separately until soft and foamy, but not hard. Add sugar mixture to egg whites. Beat on low speed of mixer until mixture begins to form peaks. Now quickly add vanilla, nuts, and food color, mixing by hand. Drop onto wax paper using a spoon. Let cool.

Pete Manly is a triple threat, writing not only in fantasy and science fiction, but also astronomy and aviation. His work can frequently be found in Analog *magazine, and Cambridge University Press publishes his astronomy books. He adds, "In aviation I have to do nasty things like write articles on the Thunderbirds. That involves flying an F-16D through loops and rolls. And yes, I have a 9G pin."*

Peter L. Manly

🍴

Aunt Jane's Seven-Layer Cookies

The recipe wasn't really invented by my aunt Jane and there are only three layers and it's more of a fudge than a cookie but after all these years, if we renamed it then nobody in the family would know what we're talking about. This is our standard dish for pot-luck suppers and picnics. The question has often been asked as to whether you can store it for several days without drying out. Nobody knows—it gets eaten first.

I usually make three batches at a time. One for the bake sale, one for the family, and one for me (put it behind the broccoli in the refrigerator and the kids will never find it). When feeding either the Mongol Hordes or teenagers, double the recipe.

Ingredients

    1 cup butter
    ¼ cup granulated sugar
    ⅓ cup cocoa
    1 teaspoon vanilla
    1 slightly beaten egg
    2 cups graham cracker crumbs
    1 cup grated coconut
    ½ cup chopped nuts (optional—I prefer the pure, unadulterated recipe)
    3 tablespoons milk
    2 tablespoons vanilla pudding mix
    1 to 2 cups confectioners' sugar
    8 ounces semisweet chocolate (you'll actually use 4 ounces but you nibble
        the rest)

Directions

Cook in saucepan until blended: half of the butter, all of the granulated sugar, cocoa, and vanilla. Add the egg and cook 5 minutes, or longer, stirring occasionally. Then gradually add the cracker crumbs, coconut, and the optional nuts. (This will be awfully dry, so you'll have to stir very hard. Show it who's boss . . .) When cool enough, press with your hands into a 9-inch square pan or the equivalent and let stand for 15 minutes.

Meanwhile, cream the remaining butter with a fork until soft and fluffy. Gradually add the milk and the pudding mix, and once these are blended, add the preferred amount of confectioners' sugar and mix until smooth. Spread this over the first layer and refrigerate another 15 minutes.

Melt the chocolate for the top layer. I have gotten best results by breaking it into small pieces and melting in a conventional oven at 250 degrees (but then, I don't own a microwave). Add a little water if necessary to make it spreadable. Spread the chocolate on top and chill, preferably overnight. One might want to score the top layer as it is hard to cut when it is hardened.

Enjoy.

Ardath Mayhar began writing science fiction and fantasy novels at the age of forty-three. Since that time, she has sold 36 novels and placed dozens of short stories in magazines and anthologies. Recent books include Hunters of the Plains, *a prehistoric fantasy,* Shewfoot Sally and the Flying Mule and Other Tales from Cotton County, *and* Through a Stone Wall, A Book on Writing. *She is presently working on more historical novels.*

Ardath Mayhar

🍴

How (and Why) to Dress and Prepare Texas Armadillo

The Texas armadillo is a perfectly edible animal, as I discovered when my family moved from Oregon back home to East Texas, otherwise known as Poor Man's Country. Our first winter after the move saw us fulfilling that prophecy.

My son Frank, having rheumatic fever at the time, slept fitfully. When an armadillo would begin scraping along the foundation of the cabin in which we lived, he would rise, take the .22, shoot it, and hang it in a tree to drain until morning.

Then I would begin my preparations. The armadillo is the cleanest animal I have ever dressed out; the stomach is usually filled with roots and bits of grass, easily removed when you clean it. It is getting to the creature that is the problem.

The upper shell is not the difficulty it might seem, for a sharp knife can be slipped around between shell and meat without much trouble.

The underbelly, however, is covered with incredibly tough hide that is covered, in turn, with coarse hair filled with grit and sand from its digging. Hosing down the thing before beginning to clean it is always a good idea.

It is in disjointing it that things get difficult. A hatchet, I found, is the best way to take apart its legs, whose joints seem to be connected in a manner that no man (or woman) is intended to put asunder. The entire body can be used in roasting, or the haunches and shoulders when boiling. There isn't enough meat on the ribs to make it worthwhile to remove it.

Once the meat is cleaned, you can either roast it or boil it with dumplings. The meat is very tender, and a coating of salt, pepper, sage, or other favorite seasoning, along with a bit of flour, holds in the juices as it roasts. I use a covered roasting pan, just as I do for beef or pork.

For dumplings, cut the meat into 1-inch chunks, boil until tender, with salt and pepper (and poultry seasoning, if you like that) to taste. Then add flour dumplings (I use a biscuit recipe, leaving out the baking powder) and simmer, uncovered, until the dumplings are done.

Although this sounds strange, we actually ate a number of armadillos during the winter of 1975–76 and found them very tasty. Do wear rubber gloves while cleaning the creature, by the way, as there have been instances of leprosy being contracted by weird people who like to wrestle the animals. Cooking entirely eliminates the problem. (Cook the armadillo, I mean. The wrestler might be a bit tough.)

I sincerely doubt you can find armadillo in any butcher's shop, but an armadillo hunt might be a good way to learn how to hunt an alien. They are about as alien as you can get.

Science fiction readers need no introduction to Anne McCaffrey, the premiere woman science fiction writer of our day, with more than 20 million books in print in English alone. Her classic novels include the Pern series and many, many others.

This is the second cookbook she has edited.

Anne McCaffrey

¶D

Colcannon

One of the major myths about Ireland deals with cabbage, potatoes, and carrots being the staple of the diet. No longer true—but that doesn't mean such estimable dishes as Colcannon should be allowed to be forgotten. I find it a sturdy meal that is very satisfying.

I must also point out that up until the English started taking over ancestral lands, the Irish were the best nourished race in Europe, having learned to use to advantage all the ecologically sound items nature provided along with the rain and the green. Reliance on one crop, the potato, ruined that balance.

Ingredients

6 mashing potatoes (one can use SMASH, but that's obscene)
1 head of cabbage, green, white, or red
1 head of kale
1 medium-size onion
2 medium-size carrots

Directions

Peel and boil the potatoes until soft enough to mash with milk, butter, and the usual seasonings.

Slice the cabbage/kale fine and allow to come to the boil. Use sufficient water to soften it. Don't turn it into sludge.

Sauté the onions until transparent. Slice the carrots into small portions and cook until soft.

Combine the mashed potatoes, cabbage/kale, and other vegetables well and turn into oven/microwave dish. Bake for at least 30 minutes in the oven at 350 degrees or 15 minutes in the microwave. Serve with lots of butter and/or sour cream.

Makes an excellent, hearty midwinter dish and can be reheated and served until the supply is gone.

Cynthia McQuillin's first sale was to The Keeper's Price, the first Darkover anthology, in 1978. Marion Zimmer Bradley had run a Darkover short story contest and was so impressed with the quality of the stories she received that she talked Donald A. Wollheim of DAW Books into publishing an anthology of the best entries. Cynthia knew nothing about this at the time, but you can imagine her joy and amazement when she received a letter from Marion Zimmer Bradley asking to buy her story for a DAW anthology. She is still writing both fiction and music, and she has since become resident cook for MZB and Greenwalls.

Cynthia McQuillin

MZBeans

Greenwalls, Marion Zimmer Bradley's household, can be a very interesting and hectic place to live. People come and go at odd hours, and we often have unusual and well-known visitors—many, but not all of them, writers. One of our dinner parties included the Romanian National Ice Skating Champion and his trainer. Because of Marion's desire to help young writers, artists, and musicians, Greenwalls has truly become a haven for the arts. Of the five current residents, four are writers, three write music, and two dabble in art, but we manage to cope with the excitement and attendant upheaval that so much creative energy can generate.

Like most writers, we all have passionate and widely varying opinions about everything that concerns us, including what constitutes a balanced diet, and the definition of words like "spicy" and "bland." As you can imagine, coming up with a meal that everyone will enjoy can be quite a challenge. Over the years I've turned my imagination and ingenuity kitchenward and managed to come up with a variety of dishes that everyone can and will consume, often with gusto.

Of all the dishes I've invented, Marion's favorite seems to be a nourishing, hearty soup which I call, in her honor, "MZBeans." It's high in fiber, low in fat and salt, easy to make, and downright delicious.

Ingredients

    1 pound low-salt, turkey ham
    1 large onion, coarsely chopped
    1 cup celery, sliced
    1 cup green cabbage, coarsely chopped

1 cup carrots, sliced
1 bag frozen lima beans, thawed or three cans of lima beans drained*
1 tablespoon low-salt soy sauce
3 or 4 bay leaves
1 teaspoon garlic powder

Directions

Combine all the ingredients, except the garlic powder, in a good size pot; then cover with water and bring to a boil. When the water boils stir in the garlic powder. Cover the pot and turn the heat to medium. Simmer for about 30 minutes, or until the beans and vegetables are done to desired tenderness. You should stir the mixture occasionally as it cooks to distribute the flavor of the bay leaves evenly throughout. When the beans are done, remove the bay leaves and serve with any good bread. The total preparation time is about 1 hour and it serves 5 easily.

*Note: Canned beans often have added salt. If salt is not a consideration, you may use the liquid from the beans to add a beanier, saltier flavor. Likewise, if salt and fat are not a consideration you may use ham, Canadian bacon, or smoked ham hocks instead of low-salt turkey ham.

Spiderfish Stew

Like many other writers, I started out in fanzines. My first published story appeared in *Starstone*, the fiction zine that the Friends of Darkover published many years ago under the auspices of MZB. Marion was the editor and read all the submissions herself, just as she does today for *Marion Zimmer Bradley's FANTASY Magazine*. One of the great joys in her life is discovering and nurturing new talent, and I feel lucky to say that, late bloomer though I've proved to be, I am one of Marion's fledglings. I stand in good company with the likes of Mercedes Lackey, Emma Bull, Jacqueline Lichtenberg, Deborah Wheeler, Elisabeth Waters and many, many more.

For Marion and the Friends of Darkover I include my recipe for Spiderfish Stew. It was inspired by one of my early Darkover stories, "Beyond Honor," which took place in Temora, a brawling seaport mentioned in the Darkover novels. Marion never really described the town, but I rather imagined it being like New Orleans in the early days. As I wrote, I envisioned the inhabitants dining on exotic seafood stews and crisp, spicy fried fish, and since crawfish—also known as langostino—is the only crustacean I can eat, I chose to use it as the basis of my stew, calling it Spiderfish.

Ingredients:

    1 medium-size onion, chopped
    1 cup celery, chopped
    ½ cup dry sherry**
    2 cups water
    1 tablespoon soy sauce***
    1 teaspoon sugar***
    1 tablespoon gumbo file
    1 tablespoon bouquet garni
    ½ teaspoon garlic powder
    2 tablespoons seasoned Italian breadcrumbs
    1 pound spiderfish tails*, cleaned and shelled

Directions

    Into a medium-size pot put chopped vegetables, sherry, water, and soy sauce. Bring mixture to boil then add sugar, gumbo file, bouquet garni, garlic powder, and breadcrumbs. Turn heat to medium and simmer till vegetables are tender, stirring occasionally. Return mixture to boiling then add the spiderfish; reduce heat immediately and allow to simmer for 5 minutes, stirring occasionally. Remove from heat and let stand for 30 minutes before serving so that the flavors may mingle. The mixture may be reheated, but the longer you cook it the smaller the spiderfish will become. The stew, which is technically a gumbo, may be served over rice in the traditional southern style, or served as is with a hearty bread.

    It takes about 1 hour to prepare and serves 5 to 6 appetizer portions, or 3 to 4 main course portions.

----

*On Terra substitute crawfish or langostino.

**Do not use cooking sherry, which has salt added to it.

***For those wishing a low-salt and sugar dish, use low-salt soy sauce and use a sugar substitute. (Add one packet while the mixture is cooling, *not* while it is cooking.)

Martha Millard is best known as one of the premiere literary agents in the science fiction field, representing William Gibson (among other stellar talents). Here she contributes a recipe she discovered in a Gibson manuscript.

Martha Millard

ᵞᴰ

William Gibson's Unnamed Pineapple Snack

Encountering this delicacy while reading the manuscript of *Count Zero* in 1985, my mouth watered, and every time I make it I think of a beach in Mexico, bright sun, and cyberspace. It's Gibson's recipe, though whether he actually makes it, I don't know. But I make it, and it's a very satisfying, refreshing snack. Healthful, too.

Directions

Take a ripe, fresh pineapple, core, peel, and slice it. Drench with the juice of 2 or 3 limes, dust with cayenne. Put in ziplock bag and take wherever you're going . . .

John Morressy is the author of 27 novels, most recently The Juggler, *a young adult historical fantasy, though he is best known for his Kedrigern series of fantasy novels. His short work has appeared in most of the major science fiction magazines. He lists his hobbies as "writing, walking, travel, and cats."*

John Morressy

🍴

Swedish Meatballs in Burgundy

It's an adaptation of my favorite recipe for Swedish meatballs in Burgundy. I've always loved that dish, but when I ran into heart problems, I had to make major changes in my diet. Out went the eggs, cheese, butter, steak-and-kidney pie, patés, profiteroles, chocolate mousse, ice cream, and other delights of the table. The traditional recipes for Swedish meatballs went with them. Along with eating so much oat bran that I often whinny, I learned to make substitutions for some of the high-cholesterol goodies. The following dish tastes great. It is not health food or heart medicine, but it's less of a threat to the arteries than the traditional recipe.

Ingredients

¾ pound ground turkey breast
¾ cup bread crumbs and oat bran, mixed
1 small onion, minced fine
¾ teaspoon cornstarch
Dash of allspice
2 egg whites
¾ cup skim milk
½ teaspoon salt
¼ cup olive oil
3 tablespoons flour
2 cups water
1 cup Burgundy
2 beef bouillon cubes
⅛ teaspoon pepper
1½ teaspoons sugar
Gravy Master

Directions

Combine meat, crumbs, onion, cornstarch, allspice, egg whites, milk, and ¼ teaspoon salt; shape into about 24 to 30 balls.

Brown well in the olive oil and transfer to a platter.

Stir flour into the fat: stir in water, Burgundy, bouillon cubes, pepper, sugar, and the rest of the salt; add Gravy Master and cook at medium heat, stirring until smooth.

Add meatballs and simmer for 30 minutes.

Serve over noodles. It will serve 4 to 6 people.

Some considerations

Use ground turkey breast rather than plain ground turkey.

Mix the bread crumbs and oat bran in any proportion you like, or use one or the other exclusively. Oat bran tends to make the meatballs denser and more compact. Using bread crumbs makes them softer.

If skim milk appalls you, use 1%, 2%, or regular milk. The recipe as given is for those concerned with their arteries.

Always use the best extra virgin olive oil.

Don't use great Burgundy in this recipe. Jug wine is perfectly suitable. If you have a cellar full of great Burgundies, it makes more sense to open a bottle to drink with your dinner. Doctors seem to agree that it's good for your heart. It certainly adds to the meal.

Add enough Gravy Master to make the sauce look like good rich brown gravy. Without it, the sauce is an unappetizing muddy pinkish color.

The above quantities will make enough for 4 hungry diners, 6 moderate eaters, or 8 dieters. Even if you're cooking for 1 or 2, make the whole batch and freeze what's left. It tastes just as good left over, and you don't have to do any work the second time around.

The following recipes come from the files of Chef Annie of Maison Morris. Maison Morris sits cozily at the bend of Lovers Lane, in picturesque Riverview, Florida. The permanent residents and staff of this comfortable inn include author Richard Lee Byers; landscape artist Terri Jones and her husband Mark; Debra Hicks; fanzine writer and SF media devotee Kendall "Two Mules" Morris; the cats, Patch, Jasmine, and Thursday; spider monkey Linda; horse Cody; the two mules, Neyca and Ruby; and, of course, Chef Annie Morris. As well as being the home of this rag tag rebel band, Maison Morris' is a frequent meeting place for the Stone Hill Science Fiction Association and specializes in theme and costume parties at which tasty treats are always of great importance. The cuisine is what has come in recent years to be known as comfort food: fare that is simple but satisfying to the body and the soul.

Ann Evelyn Morris

⅋

Chicken Paprikash

There are a lot of recipes around for this popular Eastern European dish but I couldn't leave any of them alone. Most required too much work and had too much fat. I've cut the work down and lowered the fat considerably without lessening the rich taste.

Ingredients

Pam cooking spray
3 pounds chicken, cut in pieces
1 (16-ounce) can stewed tomatoes
1 teaspoon minced, dried, or wet garlic
1 teaspoon dried, minced onion
½ cup chicken broth or water
2 tablespoons paprika
1 teaspoon sugar
1 teaspoon salt
½ teaspoon black pepper
1 green bell pepper, cut in half-inch strips
1 cup nonfat sour cream
Dumplings (recipe below)

Directions

Remove skin and fat from chicken pieces. Spray the bottom of a large skillet heavily with Pam cooking spray. Heat skillet to medium heat and add chicken pieces. Cook chicken until light brown on all sides, about 15 minutes. Remove chicken to a plate. Drain liquid from canned tomatoes and pour into skillet. Mash the tomatoes up a bit with a spatula. Stir in garlic, onion, chicken broth or water, paprika, sugar, salt, and black pepper. Scrape the bottom of the pan with the spatula to loosen any brown particles that have stuck to it. Add chicken to mixture and cook on high heat until liquid begins to boil. Reduce heat to medium-low, cover, and simmer for 20 minutes. Add green pepper strips and simmer another 20 minutes. Take chicken from skillet and place on serving platter. Turn off heat and nonfat sour cream to skillet, stirring until well mixed. Pour over dumplings and stir gently to cover. Serve with chicken and spoon sauce over chicken as well.

NOTE: If you don't like green bell pepper, you can leave it out but it does add flavor. Some people just don't like the texture of it and they should substitute ½ tablespoon dried bell pepper flakes for the fresh bell pepper.

Dumplings

Ingredients

8 cups water
1 teaspoon salt
3 eggs (or egg substitute to equal 3 eggs)
½ cup water
2 cups all-purpose flour
2 teaspoons salt

Directions

Using a large pot, start the 8 cups water boiling just after you start simmering your paprikash for the second 20 minutes. Add 1 teaspoon salt to water.

In a medium-size mixing bowl, combine eggs, ½ cup water, flour, and 2 teaspoons salt to form a very soft (and sticky) dough. Drop by teaspoonfuls into boiling water and boil for 10 minutes. When done, remove with a slotted spoon or strainer to a large casserole dish. These are chewy, pasta-like dumplings. Serves 6.

¶|D

Russian Tea Cakes

Since I am sharing my recipes on behalf of Richard Lee Byers, I've used the name for these delicious cookies that his mother used. My mother and grandmother call them Butter Balls, even though they always use margarine when making them.

Ingredients

1 cup margarine or butter, softened
½ cup confectioners' sugar
1 teaspoon vanilla extract
2½ cups all-purpose flour
¼ teaspoon salt
¾ cup nuts (pecans or walnuts are best), chopped fine
confectioners' sugar

Directions

Preheat oven to 400 degrees.
In a large mixing bowl, mix margarine, ½ cup confectioners' sugar, and vanilla. Stir in flour, salt, and nuts. Shape dough into 1-inch balls and place on an ungreased cookie sheet. Bake until set but not brown, about 8 or 9 minutes. Roll in confectioners' sugar while warm. Cool. Roll in confectioners' sugar again.

¶|D

Pink Lady Salad

This fruit salad is very versatile. It can be used as an opening course, a side dish for the entree, or as dessert. What more could you ask for from one simple recipe?

Ingredients

   8 ounces softened cream cheese
   1 regular-size tub nondairy whipped topping
   2 (16-ounce) jars fruit cocktail, juice drained
   2 (10-ounce) jars red maraschino cherries, juice drained
   1 cup walnuts or pecans, chopped

Directions

   In a large mixing bowl, stir together softened cream cheese and nondairy whipped topping until mixture is fairly smooth. Fold in fruit cocktail, maraschino cherries, and nuts. The cherries will turn the cream cheese and whipped topping a light, pleasant pink. Keep refrigerated till serving. Makes 10 to 12 generous portions.

Marianne Nielsen is the former General Editor of On Spec: The Canadian Magazine of Speculative Fiction. She is currently an Assistant Professor of Criminal Justice at Northern Arizona University, where she usually writes textbooks, book chapters, and conference papers . . . and occasionally sneaks time to write a science fiction story. She admits to having edited, a long time ago, two Canadian fannish cookbooks: Stir Wars and The Entre Strikes Back. She must share our passion for desserts, since her Chocolate-Stuffed Pears recipe was among the first we tried in this volume . . . and it's as delicious as it sounds!

Marianne Nielsen

🍴

Chocolate-Stuffed Pears

This dessert is a favorite to serve to friends who are allergic to the ASA found in most fruits and alcohol. ASA-less fruits are very few in number and include (I'm told) pears, mangoes, and papaya.

The best things are simple and a touch messy.

Ingredients

4 pears, not too ripe
1 bag good quality semisweet chocolate chips (e.g., Bakers)
½ cup water

Optional (in any combination)

whipped cream (with a touch of vanilla extract and sugar)
toasted flaked almonds
vanilla ice cream

Directions

Core the pears generously. Do not go all the way through to the bottom. Fill the pears with the chocolate chips. Place the pears in a deep, covered baking dish. Pour in water. Sprinkle in more chocolate chips (about a cup). Bake in a 325-degree oven for about an hour, or until pears are tender to the fork.

Remove pears and stir chocolate mess in the baking dish bottom with a fork. Serve pears individually in deep bowls. Spoon over each pear the thick chocolate sauce from the bottom of the baking dish. Garnish with any or all of the following: whipped cream, ice cream, toasted almonds, and, I suppose, if you insist, more chocolate chips.

🍴

Lemon-Thyme Chicken

Ingredients

2 chickens (or cut-up chicken parts to equal)
margarine or butter
1 tablespoon dried thyme leaves
½ cup water
3 to 4 lemons, sliced

Directions

Wash and cut up chickens into serving sizes. Remove skin. (Best-selling writers can afford to buy their chicken already prepared.)

Place chicken in uncovered baking pan (13 x 8-inch pan is usually big enough). Pack tightly in a single layer. Dot chicken pieces with margarine. Sprinkle thyme over chicken pieces. Pour water into pan. Place lemon slices over the chicken pieces so that the chicken is completely covered.

Bake in 375-degree oven for about an hour or until the chicken is tender. The lemon slices will dry out and turn black. This is normal, and you don't eat them anyway.

Serve with pasta or rice. Some people like the degreased chicken-lemon juice on them. It's excellent hot, but it tastes even better cold. Very good picnic food and as leftovers.

Serves about 6.

Larry Niven will probably always be remembered as the author of the classic novel Ringworld and its sequels. He writes: "I have written fiction at every length; and speculative articles, speeches for high schools and colleges, television scripts, political action in support of the space program, a total revision of the background universe for DC Comics' Green Lantern, and (with eight others) the Malibu Graphics Multiverse." He lists his interests as "Science fiction conventions. Computerized games. AAAS meetings and other gatherings of people at the cutting edge of the sciences. Comics. Filksinging. Yoga and other approaches to longevity."

Larry Niven

⑂◗

Catfish and Red Meat Flavoring

The Krups Type 708 Household Mini Food Processor is a device like a tiny Cuisinart. It purees spices and other flavorings. Look for it.

Catfish: Whirl some pecans in the Krups 708 until coarsely ground. Roll the catfish in pecans and sauté. Simple. Effortless.

Red Meat: Europeans generally add spices to butter and keep that around to flavor steaks and such. You don't need the butter. Just put lemon peel (yellow only, no white stuff), black pepper, garlic cloves, and considerable parsley into the Krups 708 and puree. What you get is nearly dry. Keep it in a jar. Rub it into any red meat with a knife or your hands before broiling (or barbeque.) It's great on a triangle tip or a crown roast.

Jerry Oltion has been a land surveyor, deejay, stone mason, oilfield worker, forester, gardener, printer, proofreader, computer consultant, and garbage truck driver. For the last fifteen years, he has also been a writer.

He even cooks a little in his spare time.

Jerry Oltion

🍴

Liquid Nitrogen Grapefruit Sorbet

A bunch of my friends had gathered for dinner. One of us knew how to make grapefruit sorbet in an ice-cream maker, but we didn't have an ice-cream maker. We did, however, just happen to have a lot of liquid nitrogen on hand, so we decided to try that.

After some discussion of which ingredient to pour into the other (Is it acid into water, or water into acid? None of us could remember or determine what relevance it had to nitrogen), we decided upon the following procedure, and it worked first time.

Afterward we had fun freezing marshmallow chicks and blowing them up in the microwave. Nitrogen narcosis, or just weird friends? Hard to tell.

Ingredients

1 part honey
4 parts grapefruit juice
4 to 8 parts liquid nitrogen (available from oxygen or welding supply stores)

Directions

Dissolve honey in grapefruit juice. (Heating will help if it's stubborn.) Using a deep metal pan or shatterproof bowl and a wooden spoon, stir mixture while pouring nitrogen directly into it. Pour slowly and keep stirring to help aerate freezing mixture. It will look like the witches' cauldron from MacBeth—this is normal. Stop stirring when mixture freezes solid.

Allow excess nitrogen to boil off before tasting! Sorbet is ready to eat when it starts to soften again.

Some tips for handling liquid nitrogen

Wear gloves, a coat, and eye protection. Store nitrogen in thermos bottles, but do not tighten caps or excess pressure will build up. Prechilling grapefruit/honey mixture will help conserve nitrogen. Leftover nitrogen is good for freezing and shattering common household objects.

Keep a responsible adult nearby at all times; it will drive them crazy.

Diana L. Paxson is the author of numerous novels and short stories, most recently including the Wodan's Children trilogy, based on Germanic mythology.

Diana L. Paxson

⑆

Thor's Goat

Once upon a time in the days when the world was young the god Thor went on a journey, driving his cart which was drawn by the goats Tanngnóstr ("Teeth-grinder") and Tanngrisnir ("Teeth-gnasher"). When the time came to rest or the night, he stopped at an isolated farm. The farmer was a poor man, and had no food to offer, so the God of Thunder instructed him to kill the goats and cook them for dinner. But they were on no account to break any of the bones.

When dinner was done, the god took all of the bones and laid them in the hides. Then he swung his hammer above them with a blessing, and up jumped the goats, alive and well once more. Unfortunately, the farmer's son Tjhalfi had cracked a leg bone to get the marrow, and so one of the goats was lame. The god claimed both the son and the farmer's daughter Roskva in recompense for the injury, and they dwell in Asgard as his servants to this day.

Goat, like deer meat, can be tough and gamy, and benefits from similar treatment. This recipe is adapted from instructions for cooking venison in Scandinavian and Early American cookbooks. The inspiration for the goat-cheese sauce is a Norwegian recipe. Unless you use an entire goat and are careful with the bones, I cannot guarantee that the goat will come alive again in the morning, but this recipe can make a difficult meat quite tasty. When you eat it, lift a glass of beer in honor of the God of Thunder who defends humankind against the Wild Powers, and enjoy the feast.

Ingredients for the goat

> several pounds—a whole shoulder will do nicely—of goat meat
> enough marinade to cover it—
> > approximately equal portions of red wine and apple cider vinegar (hard cider or beer could also be used)
> > enough slivers of garlic to stud the roast
> > pepper or crushed peppercorns
> > 1 or 2 bay leaves
> > 1 onion, sliced

Ingredients for the sauce

1 tablespoon butter
1½ tablespoons flour
2 teaspoons raspberry or lingonberry jam
1 cup Chèvre (French soft goat cheese) or ½ ounce Gjetöst (Norwegian caramelized goat cheese) *and* ½ cup sour cream

Directions

Marinade the goat meat from 4 hours to overnight; remove from marinade and stud with garlic slivers all over. Pepper lightly and put in the oven to brown for about 20 minutes at 425 degrees.

While the meat is browning, pour out most of the marinade into a deep baking dish with a lid and strain out the onion slices. Place the browned meat in the pot and drape the onions from the marinade over the top. Bake for approximately 40 minutes per pound at 250 degrees with lid on.

When the baking is done, siphon out 1 cup of liquid, and combine in a small saucepan with 1 tablespoon butter and 1½ tablespoons flour. Stir until smooth (6 to 8 minutes on medium heat). Add 2 teaspoons jam and stir until smooth. Turn down the heat, add 1 cup Chèvre (or grate in ½ ounce of Gjetöst and then add ½ cup of sour cream). Continue stirring until the mixture is smooth and transfer to a sauce boat.

Suggested dishes to accompany Thor's goat include

red cabbage steamed with sliced apples and cumin or coriander
rutabega with butter and pepper
sliced cucumber with sour cream, garnished with dill
rye bread, butter, raspberry (or lingonberry) jam
apple cider, hard cider, "Traditional Bock" or other German beer
berry pie

Tamora Pierce was born in western Pennsylvania in 1954, has lived in various states across America, and currently resides in Manhattan. Ms. Pierce began to write when she was eleven. She has been a martial arts movie reviewer, housemother in a group home, literary agent's assistant, head writer for a radio production company, and investment banking secretary. Her published books include The Song of the Lioness quartet (Alanna: The First Adventure, In the Hand of the Goddess, The Woman Who Rides Like a Man, and Lioness Rampant), and the first three books of The Immortals quartet (Wild Magic, Wolf-speaker and The Emperor Mage). She is married to writer/filmmaker Tim Liebe, and they own two cats—Vinnie Bill and Lioness (Scrap), as well as a cross-grained budgie named Zorak.

Tamora Pierce

🍴

The Best White Bread in 12 Systems

or

What to Do Till the Next Scene Develops

This is the bread recipe my mother used, the first bread I ever made, and the best. It's also the perfect bread recipe for a writer who is working through knotty material, the kind that entails frequent breaks as you pace, mutter, rip hair out, etc. It provides plenty of opportunities to vent emotions and talk through the next piece, while turning out some concrete evidence of productive labor that doesn't involve words. This bread recipe is more work than others, but it is worth every calorie you expend.

Ingredients

9 cups all-purpose flour (I use unbleached)
2 ½-ounce cakes compressed yeast *or* 2¼-ounce package dry granulated
   yeast
1 cup lukewarm water (or Obiwarm)
1 teaspoon sugar
2 cups scalded milk *or* ½ cup milk and ½ cup cold water
4 teaspoons salt
¼ cup sugar
¼ cup shortening or margarine, melted

Directions

Sift flour, then measure. (For those perfectionists who still sift—I just dump dry ingredients together and stir with a fork until everything is intermingled.) Crumble compressed or turn granular yeast into lukewarm water. Stir in 1 teaspoon sugar and let soften 10 minutes.

Scald milk (bubbles form around the edge of the pan you scald it in).

Put scalded milk, salt, and ¼ cup sugar into 5 quart mixing bowl, cool to lukewarm (about 111 degrees). If ½ water is used, add it cold to scalded milk to hasten cooling. It doesn't make any difference to the taste if you add ½ water, ½ milk, as opposed to all milk.

Always stir yeast mixture into *lukewarm* liquid.

Add 4 cups flour, then beat until smooth. (This is where the pain begins. It helps if you think about your bad guys, if you have them, or about your publisher, editor, agent, or critics.)

Beat in cooled, melted shortening or margarine.

Add enough additional flour to make smooth, soft dough; the softer the dough can be kept without sticking to board or hands, the lighter and more tender the bread will be.

Sprinkle 1 to 2 tablespoons remaining flour evenly over board or pastry cloth.

Turn dough onto floured board, cover with bowl, and let rest 10 minutes. (Dough is very soft as it is turned from bowl; when it rests, it stiffens—it's easier to handle, and you won't be tempted to add too much flour.)

Put on your loudest rock and roll album or the score to the Kenneth Branagh *Henry V* movie. Knead dough until outside is smooth and elastic, from 10 to 15 minutes. You can knead with the heels of your hands from the center out, double the mass, then knead with the heels again. Knead by rocking the dough with your fists, folding it into its center, then pushing out again. Everybody has her/his own way to knead. It's great exercise, and you can unload a lot of frustration, or set your personal writing editor to "compose" and space out. Just remember to keep an eye on the time and on the developing dough.

Shape dough into a round. Place it in the washed, well-greased mixing bowl and turn the round over once to bring greased side up. (This prevents formation of a crust on the rising dough).

Cover bowl with a slightly damp towel or paper towels, a lid, or second bowl of the same size. Place in a warm spot (80 to 85 degrees and out of drafts—I use my oven with the heat off and the door cracked a hair) to rise to double—1½ to 2 hours. When dough rises sufficiently, the dent made when you press a finger into dough remains.

When dough has fully risen, plunge fist into center of dough, fold edges toward center to punch down. Again turn dough over until smooth side is up. Cover and let rise again until double. The second rising takes less time than the first. One rising produces a decent loaf, but a second rising produces *wonderful* bread.

After last rising, punch the dough down and turn out onto a lightly floured board or pastry cloth.

Thinking of Gaul, divide dough into 3 equal parts. Make those into rounds, then cover them with bowls. Let them rest 10 minutes, then shape them into loaves. (This rest makes dough more relaxed, easier to handle.)

Place loaves in 3 greased 9 x 5 x 3-inch pans. Cover and let rise in a warm spot (80 to 85 degrees and out of drafts; again, I use my oven) until double—about 1 hour.

Bake in a 425-degree oven for about 30 minutes. When done, the bread should be well risen with a fully rounded top or "spring." The crust should be golden brown and crisp. Loaves should sound hollow when tapped on the bottom.

Turn loaves out of pans immediately onto racks. Cool 2 to 3 hours, uncovered and away from drafts. If cooled too quickly, the crust shrivels, becomes bumpy and soft.

Note: Don't soften yeast in warm milk or mix it with shortening before you start adding flour. Fat forms a film around yeast cells, slowing fermentation. If you melt margarine in the milk as it scalds, then add yeast to that mixture when it cools to lukewarm, you'll get a slow-rising dough. Best results are had by softening yeast in warm water containing a little sugar. No shortening should be added to batter until about half of flour is mixed in.

Larry Pike is a psychologist by training and a career police officer by profession. He has been active in the martial arts for most of his life, and has black belt rank in several different disciplines. He reads, writes, tries to play the banjo, and teaches for recreation. He and his delightful (but short) Japanese wife Yumiko live in Clackamas, Oregon with their two fiendish cats, Simon (who is siamese) and Momo (who is not). He also cooks.

Larry C. Pike

ᵞ𝔻

I've never been afraid of cooking—my mother had me making my own scrambled egg sandwiches by the time I was four—so if I get a bright idea that something might taste good, I just go ahead and try it. More often than not, I'm right. The only one of these that has a story behind it is the quick chili. I developed a sudden craving for chili one day, but didn't want to wait the two days it takes to make "real" chili. (You know—soaking the beans over night, simmering all day, etc., etc.) So I went to the supermarket and walked up and down the aisles with a cart, dumping in anything that looked like it might contribute. Got home, stirred it up, and an hour and a half later was amazed at how good it was. Be careful if you use the hot salsa, though. My buddy Ron, inventor of the mustard recipe, is a hot food freak. Three spoonfuls of the hot salsa kind had him sucking cold water directly from the tap.

ᵞ𝔻

Larry's Quick Chili
(Basic Recipe)

Ingredients

    1½ pounds extra lean ground beef
    1 package (5 or 6) Louisiana hot sausage
    1 large white onion, chopped
    1 tablespoon (more or less) Nature's Seasons (to taste) (Nature's Seasons
        is a seasoning blend available at most supermarkets)
    lots of garlic powder
    1 whole jar Spice Islands Chili Seasoning (*not* chili *powder*)
    2 large (family size) cans Campbell's tomato soup

3 large cans red kidney beans, drained and rinsed

1 large (16-ounce plus) jar hot salsa (This makes it HOT!—and when I say HOT! I mean **HOT!** Medium salsa is okay, too. Using mild salsa is for weenies. I like Pace HOT Picante sauce, myself.)

Directions

Use a large kettle or dutch oven because this recipe makes a bunch. Fry up the ground beef, sausage, and onion until the beef is browned and the onion is clear. Season with Nature's Seasons and garlic powder. Add chili seasoning, soup, beans, and salsa. Taste and adjust seasonings. Be lavish with the garlic. Simmer at least an hour, stirring frequently because it wants to stick to the bottom of the pan and burn if the heat is too high. It is better after spending the night in the fridge, of course.

Goes really good with cornbread.

🍴

Larry's Famous Chicken 'n' Dumplings

3 pounds boneless chicken breasts, cubed (If you're cheap, use a whole chicken. Skin the bird and remove as much fat as you can, dismember the poor thing, then proceed. After the "simmer for about an hour" step, let the whole shootin' match cool, yank the chicken parts, skim whatever fat is left off the top of the liquid, then peel the meat from the bones and put it back into the pot. Proceed with the recipe. Makes it take longer, but if you like dark meat, it might be worth it.)

1 medium white onion, chopped

Nature's Seasons to taste

2 teaspoons garlic powder (or more!) (Ain't no such thing as too much garlic. Keeps the vampires away!)

about 3 medium- to large-size carrots, peeled and sliced

about 3 big celery stalks, sliced

1½ teaspoons thyme

1½ teaspoons sage

chablis to cover

3 cups Bisquick

a couple of heaping tablespoons (more or less) dried parsley (fresh is better if you want to be fancy)

3 cups milk

1½ tablespoons Kitchen Bouquet

Directions

Sauté chicken and onion in a little butter until lightly browned. Add Nature's Seasons, garlic, carrots, celery, thyme, sage, and cover with chablis. If covering takes more than the whole bottle, add water to make up the difference.

Simmer for about 1 hour or until the meat falls apart.

Make dumplings per recipe on Bisquick box, plus the couple of heaping tablespoons of parsley. The dumplings should be a "serving spoon" size each. Put dumplings on top of simmering chicken stuff. Cook uncovered 10 minutes, then cover and cook another 10 minutes. Take dumplings out. Add about 1½ tablespoons Kitchen Bouquet and stir. (The dumpling dough will thicken the broth of the stew.)

¶D

Larry's Famous Curried Rice

Ingredients

1 large white onion, chopped
⅓ cup margarine
1 pound small shrimp, peeled and deveined (You can also use cubed chicken, pork, beef, lamb(!), or any combination of the above.)
3 cups rice
Nature's Seasons to taste
¾ jar Spice Islands Curry Powder
1 tablespoon black pepper
1½ teaspoons garlic powder
2 cans Campbell's chicken broth
enough water to total 5 cups
2 tablespoons Louisiana hot sauce
2 teaspoons soy sauce

Directions

Sauté the chopped onion in the margarine until it begins to clear. Add the meat and brown slightly, and then add the rice and sauté it for a minute or two. Add the Nature's Seasons, curry powder, pepper, garlic powder, and stir into the rice and meat mixture. You may have to add a little more margarine if the mixture looks too dry. Stir in the broth and water, Louisiana hot sauce, and soy sauce. Stir well, cover, and bring to a boil.

Reduce heat to a low simmer and let steam for 30 to 45 minutes without uncovering.

Ronbo's Magnum Mustard

Ron Bishop is responsible for this one.

Ingredients

6 ounces (2 cups) Dry Mustard
¼ cup cold water
½ cup cider vinegar
⅓ cup salad oil
½ cup firmly packed brown sugar
½ teaspoon salt

Method of Mixing

Gradually stir the mustard into the water until no lumps remain. Let the mix stand for at least 10 minutes to remove bitterness. Blending with a wire whisk (or electric mixer on medium speed), add vinegar, then the salad oil to the mustard and water mixture. Add brown sugar and salt, then beat until smooth. Spoon into glass or ceramic jars. Keep refrigerated.

If you want it hotter (!!) add a little less brown sugar and a little more (about a teaspoon) mustard.

This stuff will definitely light your fire.

Ace G. Pilkington, who earned his doctorate in Shakespeare at Oxford University, is Professor of English at Dixie College and Literary Seminar Director at the Utah Shakespearean Festival. His poetry has appeared in all of the major science fiction magazines, and one poem, "The Robots' Farwell to the Master (For Isaac Asimov)," won the Readers' Choice Award for Isaac Asimov's Science Fiction Magazine for 1992. His articles and short stories have also appeared in the United States and England.

Ace G. Pilkington

¶🍴

Orion Raummilch Rolls

One of the peculiarities of space travel is its effect on certain Earth foodstuffs. Milk, for instance, can acquire the approximate consistency of yogurt, a cobalt blue afterimage when one looks away from it, and a slightly exquisite aftertaste. Orion spacers use a Graustark clamp to cut out the Raummilch rolls, which adds the optical illusion of concentric circles to the cobalt afterimage, and may convince the uninitiated that they have eaten a piece of space itself. This, no doubt, is the source of the legends about the rolls, almost all of which are, of course, untrue.

Ingredients

    2 cups scalded milk
    4 cakes yeast
    ¼ cup whey
    ¼ cup honey
    2 cups Orion Raummilch (Yogurt may be substituted.)
    ¼ cup melted butter
    ½ teaspoon baking soda
    9½ cups flour
    1 teaspoon salt
    ¼ cup wheat gluten

Directions

Combine ½ cup milk (slightly cooled) with crumbled yeast and 1 tablespoon honey and let the mixture stand for about 5 minutes. Combine all ingredients and mix until the dough reaches the right consistency. Punch the dough down and let it rise until it doubles in size. Punch the dough down again, then roll it out about 1-inch thick on a lightly floured board. Cut out the rolls with an egg or English muffin ring (about 3½ inches in diameter). Place the rolls on a greased cookie sheet and let them rise for about 30 minutes. Bake at 375 degrees for 12 to 13 minutes. Makes about 18 rolls.

Teresa Plowright lives on Bowen Island with her husband and three young sons. She has published a novel, Dreams of an Unseen Planet, *and short stories. She is currently working on chronicling the story of Catlantis (known today as Atlantis)—a lost civilization of advanced cats!*

Teresa Plowright

‖D

Global Tostada:
Mexico Meets the Middle East

Strangely, while we all love to let our tastebuds roam far and wide, we hardly ever mix foods from different lands. Help stamp out this culinary apartheid! As a first step toward a world where curry and wasabi and pyrogies mingle freely, tabbouleh on a tostada is a phenomenal mating. Best of all, once the tabbouleh's made, it keeps for days and even improves (up to a certain point). If you're on a writing binge, you can assemble delicious meal after meal after meal with approximately one minute's labor.

Ingredients

2 cups of bulgar wheat
3 to 4 clumps of parsley
2 to 3 bunches of green onions

Directions

So: put a couple cups of bulgar wheat in a big bowl, pour in enough water to generously cover the bulgar, and soak for at least an hour. Meanwhile, wash and finely chop 3 or 4 clumps of parsley and a few bunches of green onions. (A food processor is a definite plus.) If the bulgar ends up too wet, squeeze it in a cotton dishtowel. Then mix it with the parsley and green onion.

Now, mix together ½ cup olive oil, juice of 2 lemons, 1 teaspoon balsamic vinegar (if you've got any), 4 cloves of garlic, black pepper, and 1 teaspoon cinnamon. Work this dressing into the bulgar mixture, and play around with the seasonings if needed.

When serving, throw in some chopped tomatoes. (They get limp if they sit in the tabbouleh too long.)

To assemble the tostada: Use either soft flour or corn tortillas. Sprinkle a good layer of cheese onto one tortilla. (Pre-grated "Tex-Mex" makes this part really fast.) Lay the tortilla in a frying pan and cook at medium-low heat until the cheese melts. Try putting a little oil in the pan if you're using corn tortillas.

Once the cheese is melted, put the tortilla on a plate, throw on the tabbouleh, and add some brand-of-your-choice salsa, some lettuce and cilantro (also known as "Chinese parsley"), and some yogurt or sour cream.

This is a great meal for guests: you just keep assembling more servings, as needed. And even little kids like the tortilla-and-cheese part. If you're really desperate to save time, you can microwave the tortillas-and-cheese; but they have a better texture if melted in the frying pan.

Warning: This is definflely nongourmet cooking, and I use every cooking shortcut known to humankind.

Irene Radford has been writing stories ever since she figured out what a pencil was for. Combining a love for medieval history and a fascination with the paranormal, she concentrated on fantasy with great success: the first three volumes of her Dragon Nimbus series are now out, and two more will follow shortly. The Romantic Times even called her a "mesmerizing storyteller."

Radford makes her home in Oregon, where in her spare time she enjoys lacemaking, a skill about which she has published numerous magazine articles. She also teaches needlework and writing techniques at her local community college.

Irene Radford

¶D

Dragon Fire Curry
(From the Family of Irene Radford)

This is a recipe my merchant marine father brought back from India in the late 1930s along with several crocks of the best curry in the world. The curry lasted close to thirty years. I met Tim, my future husband, when we were down to the last few ounces of the *real* curry. When he came to dinner at my parents house for the first time, my mother served the family favorite as a special treat.

My brave Tim had never tasted curry before, but he liked Mexican food. The spice wouldn't bother him. So he took a large mouthful, thinking to compliment my mother on her cooking. His eyes bulged, his face turned red, and steam nearly rolled out of his ears. Somehow he managed to grab the large glass of ice water beside his plate and down half of it without choking or spitting out the curry. He emptied his glass of water and mine too before he finished his dinner.

Less than a month later, I had a family heirloom engagement ring on my hand and Dragon Fire Curry has become a standard into a second generation.

When our son, Ben, was about a year old and just beginning to talk, the curry dish inspired his first word: "More."

We had had one of those typical toddler days of constant irritation and whining on his part and mine. We were dining with my parents again and curry was on the menu. To give me a break from the baby long enough to eat something, my mother held Ben on her lap, feeding him mouthfuls of plain rice. He continued to fuss and complain, especially when his portion of rice was gone. Mom dutifully tried to get him one more spoonful of rice that wasn't loaded with curry. Try as she might, some of the grains were yellow, but only a little. Hopefully, the spice was diluted enough not to upset his tummy.

One bite and dragon fire lit Ben's eyes. He pointed and gurgled in delight. "More," he said. "More, more, more." Before we'd left the table, Ben spoke his second word, "Milk." He hasn't shut up since.

Fifteen years later, Ben made an observation about my growing collection of dragon figurines that spawned *The Glass Dragon*, the first of the Dragon Nimbus series. The night I sold the series I served Dragon Fire Curry for dinner.

Ingredients

½ medium onion, diced
3 tablespoons cornstarch
3 cups skim or lowfat milk
2 tablespoons curry (at least)
½ teaspoon ground ginger
1 teaspoon salt (optional)
1 pound cooked shrimp meat
2 hard boiled eggs, sliced (optional)
1 tablespoon lemon juice
2 cups cooked rice
condiments
raisins
peanuts (lightly salted are best)
shredded coconut
chutney
diced pineapple—fresh or canned

Directions

In a heavy saucepan, sauté onion until translucent, in just enough butter or margarine to keep from burning. Mix cornstarch into the milk and add to the onion. Cook over medium heat until thick, stir frequently to keep from burning. Add curry, ginger, and salt. Stir in shrimp. Simmer about 20 minutes while the rice cooks. Add a little more milk if it becomes too thick. Add hard-boiled eggs and lemon.

Serve over rice with desired condiments.

Peas, fresh or frozen never canned, make a nice side dish, as does a tossed green salad.

Sherbet or sorbet for desert will help clear the palate.

Pamela Sargent won the Nebula Award, the Locus Award, and has been a finalist for the Hugo Award. Her science fiction novels include The Golden Space, The Shore of Women, Venus of Dreams, Venus of Shadows, and The Watchstar Trilogy. Earthseed, her first novel for younger readers, was named a 1983 Best Book for Young Adults by the American Library Association, and she is also the author of Ruler of the Sky, a historical novel about Genghis Khan told largley from the points-of-view of women. Among the anthologies she has edited are Bio-Futures, Afterlives (with Ian Watson), and the Women of Wonder series of science fiction by women.

George Zebrowski, an Austrian-born writer of Polish descent, is equally accomplished as a writer and an editor. His novels include The Omega Point Trilogy, stranger Suns, The Killing Star (written with Charles Pelligrino) and Macrolife. His anthologies include the Synergy series and several volumes of Nebula Award-winning stories.

Pamela Sargent

with the aid and advice of

George Zebrowski

🍴

Barszcz (Polish Beet Soup)

Barszcz is a clear beet soup that is the Polish version of borscht. It is traditionally served during holidays, often with uszka, tiny meat dumplings that might be called the Polish equivalent of wontons.

I offer the following recipes with some trepidation. The only way I could get them was to take notes while following Anne Krutol, a formidable cook who is also the mother of George Zebrowski, around her kitchen while she prepared barszcz and uszka. (Anne is one of those people who doesn't use—or particularly need—a cookbook.) Learning how to prepare this soup and the dumplings also required an apprenticeship. For at least a couple of years, whenever George and I were visiting his mother during holidays, I did little except assist in making the uszka, a process that often kept us up until the wee hours, and pick up pointers by observing Anne at work. And it's only fair to warn anyone who tries making this dish that if you succeed in preparing it properly, your family and friends are going to plague you with persistent requests to serve barszcz and uszka even if they are people who dislike beets.

In all the years I've served barszcz, I've encountered only one person who didn't much care for it.

You need a food processor to make barszcz and uszka, and even then you'll spend at least a day at the job. I usually take two days (one reason I prepare this stuff only once a year) and also make large enough quantities to store in the freezer (both the soup and the dumplings can be frozen). Anne uses an old-fashioned meat grinder and mixes the dough by hand, but I come from a less rugged tradition. She also manages to look glamorous throughout the preparation of barszcz and uszka (Anne looks something like a cross between Marilyn Monroe and Zsa Zsa Gabor), something I have never accomplished.

In early 1993, my friend Jack Dann became convinced that I was going to be a Nebula finalist that year for my novelette "Danny Goes to Mars." I was equally convinced that he was wrong, and—since Jack is a major barszcz fan—bet him a couple of bowls of barszcz and uszka that I wouldn't be in the running for the Nebula. It seemed a safe bet; in twenty-two years of writing, I had never been a finalist for any award. When, much to my surprise, I got on the final Nebula ballot, I foolishly bet Jack that, if I actually won the award, I'd follow the barszcz with *bigos*, a politically incorrect dish that is a Polish hunter's stew. (Interested readers can find my recipe for bigos in *Her Smoke Rose Up from Supper*, one of the cookbooks published to benefit the James Tiptree, Jr., Award Fund.) So of course I won the Nebula, and then a Locus Award, and became a Hugo finalist, so this bet with Jack kept escalating—I think it was going to be a six-course meal for him if I won the Hugo Award. Luckily "Danny" lost the Hugo, or I'd still be in the kitchen.

Ingredients

> 8 quarts of water
> 1 pound of beef (chunks of chuck, the kind used in a beef stew)
> 1 soup bone
> 1 large onion
> 5 scallions or green onions, white part only
> 4 fresh beets or 1 can canned beets (fresh beets are preferable, but canned beets can be used if you're desperate)
> 2 or 3 parsnips
> 3 turnips
> 4 carrots
> 4 or 5 stalks of celery
> salt
> 5 or 6 dried Polish mushrooms, dried shiitake mushrooms, or dried black Chinese mushrooms

2 to 3 tablespoons fresh dill weed or 2 to 3 teaspoons dried
2 tablespoons parsley, chopped (optional)
1 lemon

Important tip: When you cook the soup, you may use a metal pot, but *do not* store the soup in it. Store it in a porcelain pot. Barszcz, along with its accompaniment, uszka, may be frozen for future use, but store the soup and the uszka in separate containers. When you heat the frozen soup, do not add the frozen uszka to it until the soup is hot; you'll know the uszka are cooked when they are floating on the top of the soup.

Directions

Put the water in a pot. Put in the beef and the soup bone. Cook, letting it simmer for at least 1 to 2 hours, and skim off the fat that will form on top. (Skimming the fat is important; you want a clear soup when it's done.) Peel the onion and add it to the soup. Peel the scallions, halve them, and add them to the soup.

Peel the beets and grate them—a coarse grating, not fine. (If you are using canned beets, they'll be a little gooshy, but that's all right.) Peel the parsnips and turnips, and cut them into quarters. Peel the carrots, and cut them into bite-size pieces (about an inch long). Wash the celery and cut stalks into two or three pieces.

Remove the soup bone from the pot, skim any fat that's left off the top, and add beets, parsnips, turnips, carrots, and celery. Add 1 to 2 tablespoons of salt (I usually go easy on the salt here, since people can add salt to taste when the soup is served). Cook all this for at least 1 to 2 more hours. While the soup cooks, keep a small pan of boiling water nearby, and add it to the soup as needed as water boils away.

Wash the dried mushrooms in cold water, then put them into a 2-quart saucepan with about 3 cups of water; bring that to a boil and then let it simmer on a very low flame for 20 to 30 minutes. Take the mushrooms out and set them aside; add the mushroomy water to the soup. Remember to keep your pot of soup only partially covered as it cooks.

When the soup is done, take out the meat and set it aside. Remove the other ingredients, except for the carrots, and use as stewed vegetables in a side dish (if you're thrifty) or throw out (if you're not). Strain the soup into a porcelain pot. Add the dill weed and the parsley. Also add the juice of one lemon. Let it simmer a few minutes, and then cool it before storing it in the refrigerator.

Making barszcz takes close to a day, which is why I strongly advise making it one day and going on to the next step, the uszka, the day after.

🍴

Uszka (Polish Dumplings)

Ingredients

Cooked mushrooms (left over from making the barszcz)
Cooked meat (left over from making the barszcz)
2 onions
½ pound butter
salt
pepper
2 eggs
½ cup fine breadcrumbs
2½ cups flour
1 cup water

Directions

Take the mushrooms and meat and grind them up in a meat grinder, or with the metal blade of a food processor. Chop the 2 onions very fine; you don't want big hunks of onion in there. Sauté the onions in the butter until the onions are gold-colored. Put just a touch of salt in the cooking onions, just a pinch or two. Add them to the meat-mushroom mixture when they're done. Add a touch of pepper to taste. Add one egg and the breadcrumbs. Mix well and set the mixture aside.

Now make dough with the other egg, the flour, and a cup of water. Mix the dough with your hands or mix in a food processor with the metal blade. Roll dough out on a board with a rolling pin, just a bit of dough at a time, and sprinkle the board with a little flour before you roll the dough. Roll that dough *thin*. Take a shot glass and make small circles of dough. Put a spoonful of the meat-mushroom-onion mixture in the center of a dough circle. Fold the circle in half, seal it closed, then press the two ends together. (Your uszka should have the appearance of tiny ears, which is what the word means in Polish.) Make sure the meat mixture is securely sealed inside each dumpling. Keep a small bowl of water nearby, so you can seal these suckers; sometimes the dough will get dry. Dip your fingers into the water, then seal.

Heat a big pot of water to a rapid boil. Put the uszka into the boiling water, a few at a time; when they rise to the top of the water, they are done. Take them out (carefully, with a slotted spoon, one at a time), put them into a lightly buttered bowl, and add a tiny bit of butter at intervals as you add uszka to the bowl, so they don't stick. Keep doing this until you have used up all your meat mixture in uszka; as water boils away, add more, but don't add uszka until the water's boiling again. If you have to, make more dough if you need it. Store any unused uszka in the refrigerator with foil or plastic wrap over the top of the bowl. If you are going to freeze any uszka, freeze them in separate containers from any frozen barszcz.

When you serve the barszcz, heat the soup up first, then add uszka. When the uszka float, the soup's ready.

🍴

Shrimp Salad

One of my earliest childhood memories is of a day when I went digging for clams with one of my uncles along the north Atlantic coast. We steamed them, but I would have been happy to eat them raw. I can't recall a time when I didn't love fish and seafood, almost to the point of preferring such delights to any other food, and my whole family was like that. Both my father, Edward Sargent, and my mother, Shirley Sargent, were seafood fans, and passed their tastes on to all their kids, and I can remember feeling mystified when I first discovered that some of my friends actually detested fishy delicacies.

My father couldn't go wrong when he took us out to Neil's Fish Fry, a little shack near the Helderberg Mountains that served the best fried clams in the world, mountains of them, with French fries and cole slaw. There was Bob and Sue's, another shack (this one in western Kentucky), that deserved to be a national shrine for its catfish. There were shrimp and filet of sole and haddock and baked perch with my mother's favorite sauce (no, I don't have the recipe for that) and bluefish with rosemary and broiled halibut and Cantonese swordfish steak (another great recipe) and scallops (all right!). On truly special occasions, once a year at most, we would all go out for lobster, an experience that helped to prepare me for dissecting specimens in college biology and comparative anatomy courses. (This was back in the Pleistocene, when a large family could go out for the occasional lobster dinner with hors d'oeuvres, drinks for the adults, and all the fixings without having to take out a second mortgage.) When people in my family are on the prowl for fish and seafood, no barrier stands in our way. My mother has scarfed down sushi in Japan, one of my brothers is familiar with many of the great clam and scallop places in New England, my sister's seafood quests have taken her up and down the Mexican coast, and I once went to a place called Ai Pescatori on the island of Burano (a short boat ride from Venice) because somebody had once mentioned its calamari and crab. I was well into my teens before I discovered that shrimp cocktail was not a traditional Thanksgiving or holiday dish. To my family, it wasn't a real holiday meal unless you started it with shrimp and cocktail sauce—heavy on the horseradish.

That "heavy on the horseradish" was my father's prescription for cocktail sauce. I inherited his preference for spicy sustenance; my father hated wimpy food. In Mexico, he always insisted on chowing down on grub that wasn't designed for bland northern palates; as a result, he spent a good deal of his time in that country drinking gallons of beer and bottled water and announcing that his mouth was on fire. Now the trouble with most shrimp salads, much as I love shrimp, is that they tend to be wimpy. The following recipe, which is a family favorite, isn't, but I've scaled back the spices a bit.

Ingredients

½ cup mayonnaise
1 teaspoon lemon juice
¼ teaspoon curry powder
¼ teaspoon chili powder
¼ teaspoon ground coriander seed
¼ teaspoon ground cumin (optional)
1 pound of cooked, peeled, and deveined shrimp
½ to 1 cup celery, finely chopped
½ to 1 cup halved seedless red grapes (you may use seedless green grapes, but red ones make for better color contrast)
5 drops Tabasco sauce
Fresh spinach or Romaine lettuce leaves

Directions

Mix mayonnaise, lemon juice, curry powder, chili powder, coriander, and cumin. Toss gently with the shrimp, celery, and grapes. Sprinkle with a few drops of Tabasco sauce to taste, if desired. Serve on a bed of fresh spinach or Romaine lettuce leaves.

This recipe is supposed to be made with homemade mayonnaise, but salmonella has put a stop to that. A safflower mayonnaise from a health food store works well, too. Of course, there's always Hellmann's (the no cholesterol variety, the low-fat kind, or the regular mayo if you like to live dangerously), with a teaspoon of olive oil mixed into it thoroughly to improve the taste.

Serves 4 normal people or 2 Sargents.

Ron Sarti's first novel, an epic fantasy entitled The Chronicles of Scar, *recently* appeared. He has completed the sequel and is working on both an SF novel and a suspense novel. Ron is a Vietnam veteran and draws upon his military experience and knowledge of military history for his writing. Currently he lives in Ohio with his wife and two children.

Ron Sarti

🍴

Starship Trooper Chili

Actually, I call this Army Chili with my friends. I served in the army two decades ago and found a version of this chili included on a mimeographed collection of recipes distributed in the base PX. It was for soldiers and their families who wanted economical but tasty dishes for the dinner table. I don't remember the original recipe, but this is close. It remains economical and tasty. Spices, ingredients, and quantities may be freely altered until the cook finds the blend that meets family (or unit) approval. Enjoy!

Ingredients

    2 to 3 pounds ground beef (ground chuck or better preferred)
    1 onion
    2 to 3 (16-ounce) cans kidney beans
    2 (29-ounce) cans tomato sauce
    1 (6-ounce) can tomato paste
    2 cups water
    1 teaspoon chili powder
    1 teaspoon salt
    1 teaspoon pepper

Directions

Brown the ground beef and drain excess grease. Finely dice onion. Strain and rinse kidney beans. Add kidney beans, tomato sauce, tomato paste, water, and diced onion to ground beef. Stir in chili powder, salt, and pepper. Simmer for 2 to 3 hours. Serve with crackers and your favorite beverage. Leftovers can be chilled or frozen for later meals, and the taste gets even better.

Steven Sawicki is a lifelong native of Connecticut and currently occupies a 150-year-old haunted house with his wife, two dogs, and a cat. He has published a number of short stories and is currently shopping around a screenplay based on Piers Anthony's novel On a Pale Horse. *His nonfiction can be found in such places as* Cinefantastique. *He adds, "I have been a lover of baked goods since childhoood and have had to work hard not to show it."*

Steven Sawicki

🍴

Whoopie Pies

My aunt, who originated the recipe as far as I know, had two endearing qualities. The first was her laugh, which, I am convinced, was copied by funhouse operators across the country. It was hearty, out of control, and genuine. It was also highly infectious. The second quality was her baking skill. Not a day went by when I visited her that she did not pull at least a half dozen different things out of the oven—pies, cinnamon rolls, breads, cakes, cupcakes, etc. Whoopies were merely the epitome of her skill. The pies are like my aunt's laughter—infectious, hearty, and genuine. One is not enough, two is the beginning of the slide to hell, and more almost mandatory.

Ingredients for cakes

> 1 cup sugar
> 1½ teaspoons baking soda
> 2 cups flour
> 1 cup milk
> 1 egg
> 5 tablespoons cocoa
> 5 tablespoons shortening
> 1 teaspoon vanilla

Directions

> Put all in bowl and mix well. Using tablespoon, drop on cookie sheets. Bake at 350 degrees for 8 to 10 minutes.

Ingredients for filling

> ½ cup shortening

3 tablespoons butter
½ cup confectioners' sugar
½ cup marshmallow creme
½ teaspoon salt
1 teaspoon vanilla

Directions

Mix well and after cakes have cooled spread between cakes, making pies.

Caution: Use only real ingredients. Don't use shortcuts or low-fat substitutes. They are meant to be heart bursters.

Lawrence D. Schimel is widely known as one of the emerging new poets and short story writers in the field. He is also publisher and editor of A Midsummer Night's Press, which produces handsome broadsides of poems by notable authors. His work, including several notable collaborations with Mike Resnick, has appeared in quite a few magazines and anthologies lately.

Lawrence D. Schimel

¶D

Emma's Mother's
Authentic Scottish Shortbread

Between my junior and senior years in college, I spent the summer learning to dance flamenco in Grandada and then backpacking across Europe. In Florence, while sitting on the steps of the post office waiting for some new-found friends from the hostel to mail their postcards, I ran into a woman I knew from school, Allie, who'd graduated the year before. She was now at Harvard getting a Ph.D. in art history and they'd sent her to study Italian as part of her degree. She had an extra room at her apartment, which I immediately and gratefully moved into. After a few days, the school where she was studying was having a dinner party, where each of the students (all foreigners learning Italian) was to make something from their native countries. Allie made simple, good-old American brownies. Her roommate, Emma, called her mother in Scotland to get this authentic family recipe for Shortbread.

Ingredients

    12 ounces butter
    1 pound flour
    6 ounces sugar

Directions

Hard to believe, but that's it for the ingredients.

Mix the butter and the flour, making sure to keep your hands cold by running them under cold water. Mix in the sugar once the flour and butter are completely blended. Butter a pan liberally (this is important!) Pour the batter in and squish it down until it's level. Fork nice fancy designs into it to give it air and make it look aesthetically pleasing. Bake on a low temperature (we were in a rush to get to dinner on time, so we had to go for more heat in less time and burned it to the bottom).

Journeybread Recipe

"Even in the electric kitchen there was the smell of a journey."
—Anne Sexton, "Little Red Riding Hood"

1. In a tupperware wood, mix child and hood. Stir slowly. Add wolf.

2. Turn out onto a lightly floured path, and begin the walk home from school.

3. Sweeten the journey with candied petals: velvet tongues of violet, a posy of roses. Soon you will crave more.

4. Knead the flowers through the dough as wolf and child converse, tasting of each others flesh, a mingling of scents.

5. Now crack the wolf and separate the whites—the large eyes, the long teeth—from the yolks.

6. Fold in the yeasty souls, fermented while none were watching. You are too young to hang out in bars.

7. Cover, and, warm and moist, let the bloated belly rise nine months.

8. Shape into a pudgy child, a dough boy, lumpy but sweet. Bake half an hour.

9. Just before the time is up—the end in sight, the water broken—split the top with a hunting knife, bone-handled and sharp.

10. Serve swaddled in a wolfskin throw, cradled in a basket and left on a grandmother's doorstep.

11. Go to your room. You have homework to be done. You are too young to be in the kitchen, cooking.

Stan Schmidt, aside from being a gourmand and a fine writer, is primarily known for his editorship of Analog Science Fiction, *the field's leading hard-SF magazine. We have long heard tales of authors being forced to divulge recipes to Schmidt . . . see Dean Ing's excellent entry earlier in this book for one example!*

Stanley Schmidt

When I bought Lee Correy's novel *Manna* for *Analog*, I had to chuckle at his description of the eclectic cuisine of the United Mitanni Commonwealth—no characteristic local dishes, but meals combining dishes brought back by travelers from everywhere else—because that's how my wife, Joyce, and I eat at home. When we travel, we try all the local specialties we can get our hands on, and sometimes bring back cookbooks in the local languages. A few years ago, while collecting story background in Jamaica (I could show you *exactly* where pages 26–28 of *Lifeboat Earth* take place), I discovered that curried goat, despite its unsavory image in the minds of many North Americans who have never tasted it, can be very good. I didn't get a recipe then, but I had acquired a taste for Indian food while in graduate school and I eventually stumbled onto an Indian cookbook from which I learned something about curries in general. At first I found myself frequently incredulous (Did she really mean *that* much red pepper, or had I overlooked a decimal?), but eventually I felt that I understood enough about the principles of blending obviously toxic quantities of spices into edible and even tasty combinations to try some experiments of my own—including several versions of curried goat that achieved notoriety throughout Tiffin, Ohio. The recipe here is one of my inventions that I think most moderately adventurous souls will like: not a true curry, but a good old American hamburger zinged up with seasonings in a more or less Indian style and some garnishings that I won't attempt to categorize.

Curried Goatburgers

Ingredients

1½ pounds ground goat (you'll probably have to grind your own goat, and you may have trouble finding it at all. I've had pretty good luck in the big ethnic markets in cities like Detroit and the Bronx. If you can't get anybody's goat, either lamb or beef will do; the flavor of goat lies somewhere in between)

2 or 3 fresh green chili peppers (such as jalapeños), seeded and finely
  chopped
1 teaspoon curry powder (plus ½ teaspoon of a good Indian *garam masala*
  if you can get it)
½ small onion, finely chopped, or ½ tablespoon dried minced onion
1 teaspoon poppy seeds
⅛ teaspoon mace
⅛ teaspoon nutmeg
½ teaspoon crushed red pepper
1 clove fresh (or ⅛ teaspoon dried) minced garlic
1 teaspoon shredded coconut

Directions

Mix all of the ingredients together. Depending on your taste, you might
or might not want to lightly toast the onion, poppy seeds, garlic, and
coconut before mixing them in; you might also want to vary some of the
amounts.

Shape the mixture into patties (3 to 6) and sauté in butter or ghee or
broil to desired doneness. Serve hot on lightly toasted bread or buns with
melted Swiss cheese and cold grape jelly or chutney.

ⅅ

Tiffin Chutney

This is a distant descendant of another recipe which I found not bad, but
rather bland. This version has about twice as many ingredients as its ancestor
and few find it either bland or overwhelming. You make it in a lightly greased
coffee can (or one of those special baking pans that some manufacturers offer
as a fancy substitute for a coffee can) inserted in a crockery slow cooker.

Ingredients

1 (20-ounce) can of apple or peach pie filling
½ cup walnuts or pecans, coarsely chopped
1 or 2 green chili peppers, chopped (with seeds removed unless you want
  it really hot)
½ cup honey
3 tablespoons vinegar
½ to 1 ounce fresh ginger, grated (or ½ teaspoon ground dried ginger)
½ teaspoon orange peel, grated

½ teaspoon dry mustard
½ teaspoon curry powder
¼ teaspoon *garam masala* (optional but desirable)
⅛ teaspoon mace
⅛ teaspoon nutmeg
½ teaspoon red pepper
1 teaspoon mint leaves, crushed

Directions

Lightly butter the inside of the coffee can or baking pan and dump in a 20-ounce can of apple or peach pie filling. Mix in ½ cup coarsely chopped walnuts or pecans and 1 or 2 chopped green chili peppers. Mix the remaining ingredients together separately and stir the resulting mess into the other mess in the can. Cover the can, put it in the slow cooker, cover that, and cook 6 to 9 hours on low setting (or 2 to 4 hours on high). Makes about 3½ cups and keeps a long time in the refrigerator.

If you're wondering what to drink with this stuff, Joyce suggests the following, which she thinks she invented (though she admits it's so simple somebody else must have invented it, too). Anyway, it tastes good and goes well with the foregoing. The version shown is nonalcoholic; if that goes against your upbringing, add an ounce or two of rum.

🍴

Joyce's Juice Concoction

Dump 1 cup chilled orange juice and 1 cup plain yogurt into a blender. You can adjust the consistency by varying the proportions, and you can add a teaspoon or so of sugar or honey if you want it sweeter. When everything you want in the final product is in the blender, put the lid on and blend on a high speed for about 10 seconds.

Sarah Smith reports that her "first conversation with my first editor, the delightful and redoubtable Robert Wyatt, seems in hazy retrospect to have been devoted largely to exchanging recipes." Small wonder she's here! Most recently she is the author of The Knowledge of Water.

Sarah Smith

🍴

Alien Eyeballs
(Sweet and Sour Pork with Pickled Grapes)

One of the recipes that Robert Wyatt gave me was for pickled grapes, wonderful things in themselves, which go really well in sweet-and-sour pork.

If you don't have pickled grapes, you can use bread-and-butter pickles or any sweet pickle.

But *do* have pickled grapes . . .

🍴

Pickled Grapes

Make these the day before. Wash and stem 1 cup green grapes. Dissolve 1/3 cup sugar in 1 cup white or cider vinegar. Fill a Mason jar or other heatproof container with the grapes, pour the sugar-vinegar mix over it, add a stick of cinnamon, let them cool, then refrigerate for 24 hours before using.

This will make more grapes than you need, a Good Thing.

🍴

Sweet-and-Sour Pork

Sweet-and-Sour Pork is good served over white rice or Oriental noodles. Start your rice first; this recipe doesn't take very long.

Ingredients

1½ pounds boneless pork
1/3 cup cornstarch

5 cloves garlic
4 small dried chilis (optional)
½ cup peanut oil

Directions

Cut boneless pork into bite-size pieces. Cover with boiling water and cook 3 minutes. (The broth can be saved and used for something else.) Drain and dry on paper towel. Coat with cornstarch (put ⅓ cup in a paper bag and shake the pieces a few at a time). Put into a wok: 5 (or so) cloves garlic, peeled and crushed; ½ cup peanut oil (you can use less peanut oil and some water, but use peanut oil); and 4 small dried chilis (optional; don't break these open unless you like S&M-style hot food. They are supposed to hang around in the finished dish to give flavor, but if you think you might chomp on them by mistake, use Sriracha sauce, Tabasco, or any hot chili oil instead).

Stir-fry the garlic and chilis in the peanut oil, then add the cornstarch-breaded pork and stir-fry the pieces gently until they are crunchy on the outside. Remove them with a slotted spoon and pile them artistically on a plate. Leave the oil, which is by now cloudy with cornstarch.

Make a sweet-and-sour sauce by stirring together the following.

Ingredients for sauce

3 tablespoons ketchup
3 tablespoons sugar
3 tablespoons white vinegar
the juice and fruit from a small can of pineapple
1 tablespoon light soy sauce
1½ teaspoons corn starch
¼ teaspoon Patak's tikka paste (optional: makes it nice and red, if you like red)
½ teaspoon Chinese black bean sauce (optional)
3 tablespoons or so of any sweet pickle, such as pickled grapes, bread-and-butter pickle, or whatever you have on hand (optional)

Directions for sauce

Pour the blended sweet-and-sour sauce into the wok and heat it with the remains of the oil. It will thicken up and become glutinous.

If you use grapes or green pickles, add them last, since the green looks rather nice when not very thoroughly mixed into a red or brownish sauce.

Pour the sauce over the crispy pork pieces. Serve immediately. Yum.

¶⫞

MJ's Lurking Zucchini Bread

This recipe comes from my sister-in-law, Mary Jane Rowan, a SF fan in Kittery Point, Maine. MJ and her husband Carroll are organic gardeners. They are constantly exposed to the peril of lurking zucchini, the kind that hide under leaves until they reach the size of Louisville Sluggers and then come out at night and eat the house.

This is MJ's cure for lurking zucchini.

Ingredients

> 3 eggs, or beaten egg whites if you value your life
> 2 cups brown sugar
> ½ cup vegetable oil
> 1 tablespoon vanilla
> 2 cups grated zucchini
> 2 cups flour
> 1 tablespoon cinnamon (or more)
> 2 to 3 tablespoons recently bought powdered ginger or fresh, finely chopped ginger (don't wimp out)
> generous amounts of nutmeg, allspice, mace
> 2 teaspoons baking soda
> 1 teaspoon salt (or less)
> ¼ teaspoon baking powder
> wheat germ, bananas, raisins, powdered milk, yogurt, and other good things

Directions

> Preheat the oven to 350 degrees.
>
> Kill your zucchini. Remove and discard seeds. Grate enough zucchini to make 2 cups.
>
> Stir the zucchini together with the rest of the ingredients until well-mixed but lumpy.
>
> Put in greased loaf pan or 8 x 8-inch pan greased on the bottom and bake about 45 minutes. Do not underbake. The ideal texture is sinfully greasy and slightly crunchy.
>
> Have friends over to tea.

Sperry's science fiction novel The Carrier—*part of his ambitious Status Quotient series—was published by Avon Books some years ago; recent short fiction has appeared in* Speculations *and the anthology* Bending the Landscape.

Ralph A. Sperry

⫪🍴

Tio Sperry's Chicken

"Tio" is Portuguese for "uncle," although the basic rice recipe is originally Greek. "Tio Sperry's Chicken" is one of the many phrases my three cats understand completely, quite independent of my cooking the meal. (My cats also understand quite a bit of Portuguese, but are unresponsive to German or Russian.)

Equipment

    1-quart saucepan
    cast-iron dutch oven, or equivalent 4-quart pot with tight-fitting lid

Ingredients

    1 small (ca. 13 ounces) can of chicken stock
    3 ounces chardonnay
    ⅓ cup scallions, chopped (roughly 3 medium scallions)
    1 tablespoon olive oil
    1 boned and skinned whole chicken breast (½ to ¾ pound)
    1 tablespoon unsalted butter
    1 cup white, long-grain rice (do not rinse)

Optional

    ¼ cup chopped parsley
    6 to 8 sliced mushrooms

Directions

Combine chicken stock, wine, scallions, and optional ingredients in saucepan and bring to a boil (but don't allow to boil), then let simmer.

Meanwhile, heat dutch oven on medium-high until drops of water sizzle off immediately. Add olive oil and swirl until the bottom of the pot is thinly coated. Sauté chicken breast 2 minutes on each side, frequently moving it about to make sure it doesn't stick. Remove chicken breast and reserve on plate.

Keeping on medium-high heat, melt butter in dutch oven. Add rice and stir constantly and thoroughly with a table fork until rice has turned a milky white—about 2 to 3 minutes (don't let rice brown).

When rice is sufficiently milky white, add simmering contents of saucepan. (Be careful, as the stock/wine mixture will erupt briefly.) Stir quickly, then put sautéed chicken breast on top. Cover tightly, reduce heat to low, and cook for 20 minutes. After 20 minutes, remove from heat and let stand another 20 minutes. (During all 40 minutes, do not remove lid.)

After second 20 minutes, remove chicken, stir rice, and serve.

Chicken serves 2 to 3 people, depending on appetite. For more, use another whole breast of equal size.

Rice serves 4 to 6 people, depending on appetite. For more, make another batch of rice following the recipe. (The ingredients for making the rice can't be halved or doubled in this recipe.)

Remarks

It takes about 15 to 20 minutes to put this recipe together, after which the only thing you have to do is remember to turn the heat off after 20 minutes of cooking.

Don't use a whole chicken breast that's less than ½ pound, or it will get dry.

Thick-cut (¾-inch or thicker), bone-in pork chops can be substituted for the chicken breast, in which case it's "Tio Sperry's Pork Chops." (Don't use thinner chops, because they'll get dry.)

Note that the recipe doesn't include salt or pepper. Salt will toughen the meat, and, given the procedure of adding simmering stock to an already hot dutch oven, pepper can become too intense. Season to taste once served.

This makes great leftovers. The cooked rice is nukable. And any leftover rice can be recycled into any other recipe calling for cooked and flavored rice (like stuffings and soups).

The rice always comes out well, provided the lid is not removed from the dutch oven for the entire 40 minutes, and it can be made on its own without the chicken breast (or pork chops).

Mary Stanton writes adult fantasy and science fantasy for young adults. She writes gourmet cooking mysteries as Claudia Bishop. Claudia can cook.

Mary Stanton

🍴

Feedback Chocolate Chip Cookies

Don't bake these cookies when you're writing a novel. You'll gain seven and a half pounds per seventy five thousand words; a half-stone if you write in the U.K., or 3.4 kilos if you write in Europe. I don't know how much you'd gain in Kuala Lampur. I've never written a novel there.

You *should* bake these cookies when your writer's group is reviewing your work and you really need good feedback. These cookies inspire both Nick DiChario (a six-cookie man) and Nancy Kress (a four-cookie woman—but she'll tell you she only ate one) to heights. I won't say heights of what.

Ingredients

1 cup pure butter, salted
a *very* generous hard-packed ¾ cup dark brown sugar
a skimpy ¾ cup white sugar
2 extra-large eggs
a generous splash of pure vanilla extract
1 teaspoon baking powder
½ teaspoon baking soda

Directions

Beat all this together with an electric beater until it's a smooth mass.

Add 2 hard-packed cups plus of bleached white flour. Then add a little bit more.

Beat in the flour with the beater except for the "little bit more." That you'll have to beat with a wooden spoon, since the dough will be stiff.

Add an 8-ounce package of chopped walnuts and a whole 6-ounce package of semisweet chocolate chips. If you're concerned about cholesterol, substitute raisins for the chocolate, but be prepared for heavy criticism in Chapter Five. Take fist-size handfuls of dough and form them into balls. This recipe should make about two dozen cookies. Bake in a 375-degree preheated oven for about 18 minutes.

Allen Steele became a full-time science fiction writer in 1988, following publication of his first short story. Since then he has become a prolific author of novels, short stories, and essays. His novels include Orbital Decay, Clarke County, Space, Lunar Descent, Labyrinth of Night, The Jericho Iteration, *and most recently,* The Tranquility Alternative.

Allen Steele

¶D

Night of the Living Meatloaf

It took a George Romero movie to make me realize that I made awful meatloaf.

When I was a reporter for a weekly newspaper, one of my jobs was to attend low-budget SF and horror flicks when they opened at the cineplexes in Worcester, Massachusetts, and write capsule reviews of them for the movie page (this was beneath the regular film critic, who reserved himself for timeless classics like *Top Gun*). It wasn't a bad gig; the tickets were free, I received press kits I could sell to a local comics shop, and I got to see every chainsaw-killer, teenager-slasher, berserk-alien movie Hollywood churned out in the mid-80s.

Anyway, one afternoon I caught a matinee of the third George Romero zombie flick, *Day of the Dead*—probably the grossest movie I've ever endured. Two hours of mutilation, dismemberment, and mindless violence. Some people dig this stuff, but I'm not one of them; I left the theater feeling sorely abused.

Then I went home and found it was my turn to cook—and the only ingredients in the fridge were the makings for meatloaf.

I made my usual college boarding house loafer, put it in the oven, wrote a one-star review of the film I had just seen, then pulled the meatloaf out of the oven . . . and discovered that I had absolutely no desire to eat something that disconcertingly resembled a prop from that movie. It was only then that Linda, who had suffered through my post-bachelorhood cooking for the past two years, gently informed me that my meatloaf was indigestible.

I swore off making meatloaf for several years, then came back to it, gradually devising a new recipe through trial and error. Since then, I have served my homemade meatloaf to family and friends with no regrets, complaints, or flashbacks to bad horror films.

Ingredients

$1/3$ pound ground beef
$1/3$ pound ground pork
$1/3$ pound ground veal
1 large egg
1 small yellow onion, peeled
2 tablespoons Worcestershire sauce (approximately)
1 tablespoon Louisiana Hot Sauce (approximately)
ketchup (to taste)

Directions

Preheat the oven to 350 degrees. After you've washed your hands with soap and hot water, take the meats and put them in a mixing bowl. Crack the egg over the meats, grate about half of the onion into the bowl, then add the Worcestershire sauce and the hot sauce.

Here comes the messy part. Using your hands (you *did* wash them, didn't you?) combine the ingredients, kneading and rolling the mixture until everything is thoroughly mixed together. Form it into a softball-size sphere, place it in a glass oven tray, then reform the sphere into a small loaf.

Rinse off your hands, then grab the ketchup bottle and plop a healthy dose over the loaf. Use a basting brush to slather ketchup over the entire loaf.

Place the loaf in the oven, then go do something else for an hour (like write a review of a bad horror movie or make mashed potatoes—same thing, really). Pull it out of the oven and cut into four thick slices.

If you wish, you may include grated Parmesean cheese, bread crumbs, and a little beer in the mix. However, I stopped adding that junk a long time ago; you can't taste 'em anyway, so why bother? And never add sliced mushrooms, which was part of my old recipe . . . they ruin the taste and look disgusting besides.

Meatloaf is something any fool can make, but good meatloaf is something that takes time and practice. Experiment with this stripped-down recipe until you get something your love will eat without hesitation.

Serves 2 to 3 people (double everything for 4 or more).

†)

Allie May's Fried Corn

This is a Steele family recipe, but it was passed to us by Allie May, the nice old black lady who was my grandfather's housekeeper for many years.

Ingredients

3 ears of white corn
1 small can of creamed yellow corn
1 cup of water

Directions

Husk the white corn, then use a paring knife to strip the kernals from the cob into a large frying pan. Open the can of yellow corn and pour it into the pan. Stir it all together, then add about a quarter of a cup of water.

Cook on medium-high heat, allowing the water to boil off, yet adding a little more now and then to regulate the temperature. If you do it right—and it will take a bit of practice before you do—you'll get a slightly blackened, somewhat stringy mess that looks like hell but is absolutely delicious.

Serves 2 to 3 people.

Del Stone, Jr. is a professional science fiction/horror writer. He is known primarily for his work in the contemporary horror field, but has also published work in the science fiction field. Del's stories, poetry, and scripts have appeared in publications such as Amazing Stories and Full Spectrum. He is single, bowls, plays tennis, takes responsibility for every hurricane that strikes the Florida panhandle, and carries a permanent scar on his chest after having been shot there with a paintball gun. He just turned forty and now pays his income tax with a smile.

Del Stone

¶D

Del's Hellfire Chili

Ingredients

1 pound ground beef
2 (15-ounce) cans tomato sauce
2 (16-ounce) cans chili beans (or red kidney beans)
1 habañero pepper (or 3 jalapeño peppers), chopped
3 tablespoons hot chili powder
1 clove garlic, chopped
½ cup onion, minced
1 tablespoon vinegar
1 tablespoon Worcestershire sauce
1 teaspoon Tabasco sauce
½ teaspoon salt
dash cayenne pepper
dash ground red pepper

Directions

Brown ground beef, draining fat. Grumble.

In a stewpot, mix tomato sauce, chili beans (including liquid), habañero pepper, chili powder, garlic, onion, vinegar, Worcestershire sauce, Tabasco sauce, salt, cayenne pepper, and ground red pepper. Bring to near-boil, stirring well.

Add ground beef. Reduce heat.

Simmer on low heat for 30 minutes.

Makes 6 servings.

Miscellany

Known primarily as a foodstuff, Del's Hellfire Chili may also be used as a personal protection substance (by hurling it into the eyes of an attacker). Nations have filled border-moats with Del's Hellfire Chili to deter intruders, and Adolph Hitler is rumored to have poured it into his ear as he was leaving his Berlin bunker. It is the only entrée to be served as a breakfast, lunch, and dinner special in Hell.

That is to say: It's hot.

Its preparation requires a deft hand, and a contamination suit. For best results, use a lean grade of beef, drained well. A brand of tomato sauce that contains chopped celery and onions (such as Hunt's Tomato Special) adds another dimension to its, er, saucy nature. Chili beans canned in a spicy stock enhance the misery. The habañero pepper is, of course, a critical ingredient, contributing an earthy flavor of heat, similar to that of magma. But wussies may substitute jalapeño peppers. An important tip: After chopping your pepper of choice, do not—repeat—*do not* touch any portion of your anatomy (most especially if nature calls at this inopportune moment) before washing your hands. For a California twist to this recipe, substitute pineapple for the onion.

Del's Hellfire Chili is best served with: a case of Foster's lager, Lake Huron, skin grafts, or a hospital intensive care unit.

Kiel Stuart claims a cookbook collection that threatens to overwhelm her house. Ms. Stuart's work can be found in such widely varied places as the New York Times, Tales of the Witch World, Muscular Development, *and* Women of Darkness. *She is listed in* Who's Who in the East *and publishes a fiber arts newsletter.*

Kiel Stuart

¶D

Curried Cocktail Walnuts

I wish I could come up with an amusing anecdote as to how I created curried cocktail walnuts. But it's just one in a neverending string of recipes I've invented over the years. Maybe there's a bit of chemist in me; when I was a little girl I used to throw acorns, salt, and ginger ale together just to see what would happen. Fortunately, most of my results are more palatable than that.

Curried cocktail walnuts is one of the easiest dishes you'll ever make, and the results are irresistible.

Ingredients

1 pound shelled walnuts
½ cup sour cream
1 tablespoon good curry powder
Optional: cayenne pepper and/or salt

Directions

Preheat your oven to 350 degrees. Grease a large cookie sheet or baking pan. In a large mixing bowl place shelled walnuts, sour cream, and curry powder. A generous shake of cayenne pepper and/or salt is optional. Mix well.

Turn the coated nuts out onto the greased cookie sheet and bake, stirring every 15 minutes or so until light brown and crisp. Cooking times will vary, but count on at least 20 minutes. Let cool and devour. Goes especially well with dry sherry or a good dark beer.

Jane Toombs, born in California but raised in Michigan's Upper Peninsula, has recently moved from upstate New York to Carson City—the result of falling in love with Nevada as well as a Nevadan. (He was also raised in the Upper Peninsula, so is a displaced Yooper like Jane—for more on Yoopers, read on!)

Toombs is the author of forty-four published books, encompassing not only the various romance genres (suspense, contemporary, historical, and Regency), but also such genres as mystery, fantasy, and horror. She writes under her own name as well as a few pseudonyms, including Ellen Jamison, Diana Stuart, and Olivia Sumner.

Jane Toombs

¶⫯

Yooper Stew

Yoopers, being the step-children of Michigan (you talk funny—where you from?), never do quite get into step with the rest of the world and we're proud of it. Though born a prune-picker (CA), I arrived in the Upper Peninsula of Michigan at three months of age and grew up there, thus qualifying me as a Yooper. Those unlucky enough to reside in Michigan's Lower Peninsula may get the cream of the state's tax money, but actually they're Trolls since they live beneath the Mackinac Bridge.

When I was young, Yoopers shot deer when they needed to (this translates to being hungry—the area's always been economically depressed) and so the basis for true Yooper Stew is venison. Since deer meat is an acquired taste for most people, I usually substitute beef.

Ingredients

1 to 1½ pounds steak (whatever is on sale—don't use prepackaged stew meat)

3 to 4 potatoes

4 to 5 carrots

½ (at least) a rutabaga (sometimes called a yellow turnip but not by Yoopers)

2 garlic cloves

½ to 1 onion (depends on size)

2 cubes condensed beef broth

pepper to taste

chopped parsley

Directions

Cut up meat, brown in hot pan, and season with pepper. Add several cups of water, the cut-up chunks of vegetables and the broth cubes. The water should almost cover the resulting mixture. Add chopped parsley and more pepper. Simmer for 2 to 3 hours. Mix presifted flour in small amount of cold water, add to stew to thicken slightly and allow to come to simmer heat once more. Can be served in soup-plates or on dinner plates. Will feed four. To expand, use more meat and vegetables. Serve with bread (Prune-Picker sourdough is great with this) to mop up the juices.

Yoopers have been known to add beer. Those who insist on experimenting may add various herbs, spices, and their favorite vegetables but the stew is tasty as is and even better the second day.

Kathy Tyers' first SF novel, Firebird, *was followed by* Fusion Fire, Crystal Witness, Shivering World, *and* Star Wars: The Truce at Bakura. One Mind's Eye *is scheduled for 1996. Her other love is music. Kathy's grandmother taught her piano, which she promptly gave up when her mother started her on flute lessons. Besides writing, she performs and records semiprofessionally with her husband, Mark Tyers, as a folk duo. She has performed on her mother's flute since 1982, and Grandma Putnam's piano is now part of the Tyers household.*

Kathy Tyers

¶⫯

Four-Generation Banana Bread from the Philippines

My grandmother brought home the hand-lettered recipe, "Banana Bread from the Philippines," in a 1950s cookbook assembled by the Assistance League of Long Beach, CA. The first time my mother (Grandma's only child) baked it, my sister and I pronounced it "much better than regular banana bread." Its aroma still stirs memories of skate keys and music lessons.

Mother was murdered in 1982, and the case is still unsolved. It broke our hearts, but it didn't break Grandma. A series of minor strokes finally left her bedridden in 1993. Now if she wakes when I visit, she often calls me by her daughter's name. I do look more like Mother every year, especially my hands and my eyes.

Recently I crossed Mother's recipe with a zucchini bread method I found in her food-processor cookbook. It came out perfectly, and it's fast enough that my Generation X son and nieces can find time to bake it.

It takes about 20 minutes preparation time, including cleanup and licking everything lickable, plus 1 hour bake time. Don't bother to clean food processor parts between steps.

Ingredients

1 cup walnuts
3 ripe bananas (or frozen and mostly thawed)
½ cup milk
2 cups flour
1 cup sugar
⅓ cup oil

1 egg
1 teaspoon baking powder
1 teaspoon baking soda
½ teaspoon salt
½ teaspoon cinnamon
¼ teaspoon nutmeg
¼ teaspoon ground cloves

Directions

Preheat oven to 350 degrees. Get out food processor and 3 small mixing bowls or large cereal bowls, rubber spatula, measuring cups and spoons, and ingredients.

In food processor, chop walnuts with blade using brief on/off pulses. Scrape out into small bowl.

In food processor, mix bananas (ripe or frozen and mostly thawed) with milk until milkshake-smooth. Scrape out into a different small bowl.

Sift 2 cups flour into one more small bowl.

Into food processor, place sugar, oil, egg, baking powder, baking soda, salt, cinnamon, nutmeg, and ground cloves. Mix on continuous cycle about 15 seconds, until smooth.

Add half to a third of banana mixture to food processor, mix about 10 seconds. Repeat with flour, then bananas, etc., and scrape down sides halfway through. Finish with flour.

Remove blade. Mix in chopped nuts with spatula.

Pour batter into loaf pan lined with aluminum foil (spray foil with cooking spray).

Bake about 1 hour, until toothpick inserted at center comes out clean.

Edo van Belkom is the author of the novels Wyrm Wolf, Mister Magick, *and* Lord Soth *plus more than ninety short stories in various magazines and anthologies. Roberta van Belkom is a children's librarian whose poetry has been published under the pen name L. L. Barrett.*

Edo van Belkom and Roberta van Belkom

🍴

Butternut Dumplings (Squash Gnocchi)

When you make this recipe a second time, you'll know from your first experience whether to add more or less flour, or more or less salt than what the recipe calls for. One recommendation: don't cut down on the cheese, it's what makes these dumplings as good as they are. Beta carotene is supposed to be good for you and anything orange is supposed to have lots of it. However, the problem is how to get the men in the family to eat anything that looks even remotely nutritious. So, I (Roberta) came up with this recipe knowing that they'd eat regular potato dumplings (except in our house they are *definitely* called gnocchi) and I heard that squash has the same properties as potatoes with the added bonus of extra fiber and lots of beta carotene. It turned out to be a hearty and healthy meal for just a few bucks.

Tips in selecting a good butternut squash

1. Look for one that is about 6 to 9 inches in length.
2. Avoid one with a very large bulb, it usually means hollow with plenty of seeds.
3. It should feel solid.
4. Test it with your fingernail. A fresh one will not keep the indentation for very long. The fresher the squash, the longer it will keep at home, especially during those long winter months.

Ingredients

1 small butternut squash
1 cup grated Parmesan cheese (Parmiggiano Reggiano is the best.)

184

2 eggs, slightly beaten
½ teaspoon salt
all-purpose flour
olive oil

Directions

Peel squash and cut in half lengthwise. Scoop out seeds and put them aside for your composter.

Cut up squash into 1-inch chunks. Place in small pot with enough water to cover squash. Boil on medium heat until cooked. (Prick with fork until tender.) Drain and place in bowl or food processor. Mash to consistency of mashed potatoes.

While stirring, add cheese and eggs. Mix well.

Gradually, ½ cup at a time, add flour. Mix well after each addition. Add enough flour to make a firm batter—not as firm as pizza dough. Stringy pieces of batter should stretch around wooden spoon.

Place a clean pot filled ¾ with water on medium-high heat. Bring to a boil. Add 1 tablespoon olive oil to the water.

Drop batter by teaspoonful into the pot (use 2 spoons—one to pick up from bowl and the other will help to roll batter off spoon and into the water). Drop enough dumplings into pot to cover surface.

When dumplings rise to surface, it means that the outer layers are done. Let boil an additional 3 to 5 minutes. (You can always do the taste test on the first few to determine doneness.)

Remove cooked dumplings with slotted spoon and place in a covered baking dish.

Repeat this process until all batter is gone. Careful not to eat too many while making them, or you will not have any left for meal time.

Just add cheese and enjoy or top with favorite sauce (meat, tomato, white or pesto — not fish).

Dumplings can be topped and left in a 200-degree oven to keep warm. Best served warm. They can also be reheated in a microwave by adding a little butter and water to pan.

⅋⑁

Book Launch Party Dip

This recipe came about when we were preparing for a party to celebrate the publication of Edo's first novel, *Wyrm Wolf*. On the eve of this party, I (Roberta) realized that I forgot to buy the real ingredients to this recipe my aunt had shared with me. So, I put together new ingredients from the items I had around the kitchen and it turned out to be great. Hope you enjoy it too.

Ingredients

1 small package frozen spinach, chopped
500 ml. (2 cups or 1 large container) of sour cream
250 ml. (1 cup or 1 large package) cream cheese, beaten
1 small onion, finely chopped
¼ green pepper, finely chopped
¼ red pepper, finely chopped
1 package vegetable (no noodles) soup mix
bread (rye, pumpernickel, and/or Italian)

Directions

Boil spinach in small pot with about ½ cup water—careful not to burn. Drain any remaining water and spread on a plate to cool.
While spinach is cooling, combine all other ingredients.
When spinach is cooled, chop and add to mixture.
Taste to see if you'd like to add salt.
Place in an air-tight container and store in the fridge overnight.

To serve

Cut up sliced rye, pumpernickel, and/or Italian bread in quarters and place on a large plate or tray. In the middle add a bowl with dip and enjoy.

⅋⑁

Twenty-four-hour Fruit Salad

This recipe serves at every holiday dinner in the van Belkom family and can vary by adding any leftover fruit you happen to have on hand. My mother-in-law has never made it twice the same way in the fourteen years I

(Roberta) have enjoyed this desert. The boys enjoy it for breakfast for days following the holiday itself.

Ingredients

1½ cups cold milk
1 large package instant vanilla pudding mix
1 cup or small container of frozen whipped topping, thawed
1 small can mandarin orange slices, drained (discard syrup)
1 can (20-ounce) pineapple chunks, well drained (keep juice)
2 cups seedless white grapes, washed and drained
2 cups colored or white mini marshmallows
top with any slice of the following fruits: kiwi, cherry, sliced strawberry

Directions

In a large bowl, prepare base by mixing milk and pudding. Add whipped topping and fold into pudding.

Add: orange slices, pineapple, grapes, and marshmallows. Fold in well.

Level mixture and cover well; refrigerate overnight.

Serve as after dinner desert.

Oh yeah, the pineapple juice . . . enjoy it as a beverage.

Joan D. Vinge is best known for her Snow Queen *series, beginning with* The Snow Queen *(for which she received a Hugo Award in 1981) and continuing with* World's End *and* The Summer Queen. *She also received a Hugo Award for her novelette "Eyes of Amber."*

Joan D. Vinge

¶D

Death by Chocolate: A Murder Mystery

(a.k.a. Chocolate Brownie Tart)

I got this recipe (renamed by me) from one of the people running a convention at which I was Guest of Honor, up in Canada. He'd made these goodies for the traditional party there, and they were so decadent I asked him for the recipe (which he got from his mother). I've noticed that when I'm Guest of Honor somewhere and men are in charge, they often like to show off their baking skills.

Ingredients for crust

1 box of chocolate wafer cookies, crushed
¼ to ½ cup melted butter

Directions

Mix and press into a large baking pan (16 x 11-inch or 13 x 9-inch).

Ingredients for center

6 ounces unsweetened baking chocolate
6 ounces semisweet chocolate
½ cup melted butter
3 cups sugar
6 eggs, beaten
1½ cups flour
nuts (optional)

Directions

Preheat oven to 350 degrees. Melt chocolate and butter, mix in sugar. Fold in eggs. Add flour (and nuts, if desired). Pour into pan. Bake about 30 minutes. Let sit for 3 to 4 hours to cool.

Ingredients for glaze

6 to 8 ounces semisweet chocolate
¼ cup whipping cream or ½ cup butter

Directions

Melt semisweet chocolate. Add whipping cream *or* butter and pour over the top. Let it set at room temperature or refrigerate, but the latter causes it to sweat. Cut into very small pieces—it is *rich*.

Prolific short-story writer Don Webb is well known to readers; his fantasy and science fiction stories can be found in most of the leading magazines and many anthologies. Currently he lives in Texas.

Don Webb

Shrimp Anarchy

Ingredients

1½ cups onion
1 cup celery
2 medium green peppers
4 cloves garlic
¼ cup margarine
2 cups tomato sauce
1 cup water
2 teaspoons minced parsley
½ teaspoon salt
1 teaspoon cayenne pepper
2 bay leaves
1 pound cleaned raw shrimp
3 cups rice (prepare separately)

Directions

Chop onion, celery, peppers, and garlic. Cook in margarine or fat for about 5 minutes. Remove from heat; stir in tomato sauce, water, and seasonings. Simmer about 10 minutes. Add shrimp, cover, and cook for 10 to 20 minutes until shrimp are pink and tender. Serve over hot rice.

While shrimp are in preparation, have your local troop perform the following actions:

1. Begin calling all local branches of the federal government and tell them that their department has come under fire in the national budget-cutting process. Advise them that the only hope for their jobs is an immediate flight to Washington to testify before the Senate finance committee. The bureaucrats will then flee their offices.

As they abandon their offices, send paint crews to rename the offices for plumbing and artistic firms. Change locks. The resulting confusion will end federal control of your area.

2. Blow up all cable TV facilities in your area. Call all local TV stations. Threaten them with destruction unless they agree to show nothing but the "What Makes Auntie Freeze?" episode of *My Mother the Car*. This will cause all but the most brain damaged among the local populace to turn off their sets and begin to think. For those who still remain addicted to the tube, there isn't any hope anyway.

3. Call up all the local schools, identifying yourselves as the local fire marshall, tell them it is time for an impromptu fire drill. Call up all firms that provide ice cream refreshments from trucks. Tell the trucks to head to the schools, that a special school holiday has just been declared and the kids will want to celebrate. Remind them to announce the holiday over their loud speakers as they approach the schools.

4. Call the local churches, synagogues, and mosques. Tell them that the largest churches in the city have started a raffle program that gives money to a random church goer. Ask them if they have a statement on how much money *they would pay* to have someone to attend their church. Tell them that all the other churches are making statements at the local radio stations. Call all the local radio stations and tell them that church groups are making a hostile march on them *en masse*. Tell the radio stations the only way to avoid religious attack is to quickly found their own religions and start broadcasting them right away. Tell them that the churches won't attack their own. This will cause the state's greatest ally in enslavement, the churches, and the state's second greatest ally, the media, to fight amongst themselves.

5. Call up local government offices and tell them that the feds are planning to absorb all their functions in a few days. Say that the governor/mayor has said that the only way folks may keep their jobs is if they picket all federal buildings, with placards marked "Power to the People!" The federals will have all left, and the arriving picketers will be picketing the locksmiths and painting crews. Call the local newspapers and ask them why all our local government is downtown picketing honest working men and women? Why is is local government opposed to Labor? Express a hope that the local newspaper will cover the story, since all the radio seems to talk about any more is religion.

6. Call the police and announce that the biggest shopping mall in town is offering a free fifty dollar gift certificate to the first two hundred police men who show up in uniform at the mall. Call all the malls and tell them

that the police are in a state of revolt and are coming to mall after mall to loot freely. If they doubt the story, call up the biggest mall and ask if the police are coming in number. Tell them that to avoid panic, they should leave the malls—keeping all the doors open—and hope that the police will take what they want and just go away. Tell the homeless in your neighborhoods that it's a good day to visit the malls for a clothing upgrade.

7. At this point shrimp will be done; go home, eat shrimp, start next batch.

8. Go to all the empty churches, synagogues, and mosques. Put large hand lettered signs on each. "Going Out of Business Sale! All furniture free for hauling." Give everyone that shows up some of those anarchists zines you've been storing for years. Numerous copies of The Stars My Destination are also nice gifts. Help people loot the churches, synagogues, and mosques. Tell each one of them, "Well we're going to have start figuring this stuff out for ourselves now." Mention that all the local government offices have gone out of business too, and that everything there's free as well.

9. Get a large electromagnetic crane, such as the kind used in car demolition lots. Use its mighty magnetic field to wipe away all records at banks, courthouses, and taxation offices.

10. Storm the electric power station. Turn all power off in the city for 23 minutes.

11. In the instability that will follow use your judgment and creativity to change a mindless falling away of the system into an individualistic small scale society unlike any that have existed in history save for our dreams. Some ice-cream would be nice too, since the shrimp burns a little.

May be served without anarchy.

Serves 4.

Catherine Wells is the author of a science fiction trilogy: The Earth Is All That Lasts; Children of the Earth; *and* The Earth Saver. *A playwright as well as a novelist, she holds a bachelor's degree in theater from Jamestown College (Jamestown, ND) and a Master of Library Science degree from the University of Arizona. She resides in Tucson, Arizona, with her husband, two daughters, a dalmation, and a tortoise-shell cat.*

Catherine Wells

Fian Flat Bread

Okay, when I got this recipe handed down from my mom it was "Finnish Flat Bread," but *fians*, sometimes called *finns*, are a legendary folk in Irish, Scottish, and Norse tales. You'll find them mentioned in the same breath with Faeries and Picts. Whenever a Scandinavian folk tale features a "Finn-wife" or "fian-wife," you know there's magic afoot!

Being of Finnish extraction (or as my siblings and I like to say, being half-Finnished), I have a few "traditional" recipes which I like to trot out on special occasions. This is one of them, and I couldn't resist the temptation of giving it a fantasy name.

So whip out your favorite white bread recipe and follow the directions; or use my family's white bread recipe below (but if you have high blood pressure, you might want to cut the salt in half!) Sorry—you can't make flat bread in your bread machine!

Ingredients

white bread dough

Directions

Divide bread dough in half for two loaves. Let rest for 10 minutes. Then flatten down to about ¾ of an inch and let it rise for 30 minutes. Before baking, prick all over with a fork, as for a pie shell. Bake on a cookie sheet in a 375-degree oven for 45 to 50 minutes. Pricking the dough and giving the gases a chance to escape gives this bread a very cakey texture, so it's great with butter and jam—and of course, a good cup of Finnish petrol (coffee).

🍴

Basic White Bread

Ingredients

½ cup warm water
2 packages dry yeast
1¾ cups warm milk (105 to 115 degrees)
2 tablespoons sugar
1 tablespoon salt
3 tablespoons margarine or shortening
5½ to 6½ cups flour

Directions

Measure warm water into large warm bowl. Sprinkle in yeast, stir until dissolved. Add warm milk, sugar, salt, and margarine. Stir in 2 cups of flour. Beat with a rotary beater until smooth, about 1 minute. Add 1 more cup of flour. Beat vigorously until smooth, about 150 strokes. Add enough additional flour to make a soft dough. Turn onto lightly floured surface and knead until smooth and elastic, 5 to 10 minutes. Proceed with instructions for *Fian Flat Bread*.

Leslie What, the self-described "Housewife from Hell," has published stories in most of the major science fiction magazines, including Asimov's Science Fiction and The Magazine of Fantasy & Science Fiction. She attended both the Clarion Writer's Conference and the Bread Loaf Writers' Conference.

Leslie What

❦

Cheese Bake Redux

Ingredients

12-pack of the world's cheapest macaroni-and-cheese box dinners from Costco/Price Club
2 sticks of margarine, or if you're feeling charitable, butter
milk
5 pounds Costco/Price Club shredded cheddar cheese packs
salt and pepper to taste

Directions

Boil as many boxes of macaroni as you can fit into your biggest pot. Mix with dry cheese sauce as directed on the package.

Nights 1 and 2: Eat without further ado. Store remains in a 36 x 24-inch institutional casserole dish, also available from Costco/Price Club. Serve with prewashed salad (comes in convenient resealable plastic bag) and bread from the family-size You-Bake Sourdough Bread Loaf Bonanza.

Night 3: To freshen, add handfuls of shredded cheese to the top layer of leftover casserole and bake until melted. Serve with instant salad and bread.

Night 4: Replenish top layer of cheese and reheat. Usually, I serve canned fruit at this time, for variation (comes in convenient case of 24).

Night 5: Butter a cake pan. Spread leftover macaroni and cheese evenly into one thin layer and drizzle cheese over the top. Cut into squares while still warm. Open 1 can from a 12-pack of chili con carne and pour over that. Top with more cheese. Serve with you-bake bread loaf and instant salad, if it's not too moldy. Or, cook the wilted salad and tell them it's German cabbage. Set aside leftover chili con carne, shredded cheese, and extra bread loaves for another meal.

꠸🍴

Chili and Cheese "Pie"

Ingredients

you-bake bread loaves
chili con carne
shredded cheese

Directions

Hollow out a couple of you-bake and fill with cans of chili. Top with cheese and microwave till hot. Serve with frozen corn on the cobbette.

꠸🍴

Baked Flash-Frozen Snapper with Cheese Sauce

Ingredients

5 pound bag of frozen fish filets
½-gallon can of nacho cheese sauce

Directions

Spread filets into buttered casserole dish and top with canned cheese sauce. Bake at 325 degrees for 45 minutes. Freeze leftovers in plastic bags for a tasty "instant" meal. Feeds 15 hearty appetites or 100 children who hate fish.

꠸🍴

"Quick" Mole

Ingredients

box of milk chocolate bars from Costco/Price Club
margarine
flash frozen chicken breasts

Directions

Brown chicken breasts in frying pan and place single file in casserole dish. Bake at 325 degrees for 20 minutes. Microwave a dozen chocolate bars and pour sauce over chicken. Serve with frozen corn cobbettes, a really big bag of chips, and one of those huge plastic jugs of salsa.

ᵞⅅ

Cooking Your Mistakes, A Recipe for Leftovers

The Basic Four, Redefining Terms

The first food group includes things that are eaten immediately. Brie, candy, steak, and popcorn are prime examples. The second food group are legally edible things that no one will eat. Foods that rate high on this list are brussels sprouts, kale, and cheeses marked down because of a "little" mold. The third food group includes those things that the children have to eat in order to get dessert, like vegetables and organ meats. The final food group, and the subject of this recipe, is leftovers.

Subdividing Leftovers Into Categories

The first category is leftovers that will at some point be consumed. These include foods like pizza, pasta salads, watermelon, and all deserts except custard.

The second category is everything else. This includes any foods you sincerely believed would be eaten, as well as foods left out to cool and then forgotten, or foods that have been refrigerated in unlabeled containers. Chief offenders are foods that have been temporarily stored because you suspected they could be combined to form another meal.

A sub-grouping of category two includes foods you knew would not be consumed but felt too guilty to throw away. Small portions of meat and fish, or large portions of rice and mashed potatoes. Cooked vegetables, slices of bananas, the other half of the grapefruit. There are foods that are predisposed toward leftoverosity. Things like eggplant; stir-fry; spaghetti; pancake batter; holiday foods, especially turkey; and canned foods that only your children find interesting. You can do nothing about these kinds of foods. Forget about it, and do what you can about the rest.

Leftovers happen. Deal with them.

🍴

Old-Fashioned Leftover Fish Pie

Ingredients

1 small onion, chopped
2 tablespoons olive oil
a few old mushrooms, chopped
¾ cup (more or less) old fish
1½ cup old rice
1 tablespoon dry parsley—or old fresh
3 hard boiled eggs, finely chopped
salt and pepper to taste
package of two frozen pie shells
4 tablespoons butter

Directions

Fry the onions in oil until soft. Add mushrooms. Remove from heat and add flaked fish, rice, and parsley. Mix well. Add eggs and seasoning to taste. Spoon mixture into defrosted pie shell and drizzle with butter. Place second pie shell on top to form crust and crimp edges. Bake in preheated 375-degree oven for 45 minutes or until crust is golden.

If you happen to have any leftover spinach or cooked broccoli lying around, you can throw in ¼ cup of that, too.

Deborah Wheeler is the author of Jaydium *and* Northlight, *and her stories have appeared in such anthologies as* Ancient Enchantresses, Sisters of the Night, *and* Star Wars: Tales from Jabba's Palace.

Deborah Wheeler

¶D

Worm Pie

Worm Pie started life as Spaghetti Pie in a cookbook, but I've changed the ingredients and instructions many times over the years. I think it's different enough to be considered original.

Ingredients

½ pound spaghetti
2 tablespoons olive oil
1 clove garlic, minced
1 pound very lean beef or turkey
½ cup each diced onion, green or red pepper, mushrooms
½ cup tomato sauce
½ teaspoon each basil, salt, whole fennel seeds
dash hot sauce
1 egg
4 ounces shredded mozzarella

Directions

While the spaghetti is cooking (according to package directions) take a large skillet, heat oil and sauté garlic and meat. Add vegetables and cook until tender-crisp, about 5 minutes. Drain off fat, if any. Add the sauce and seasonings. Remove from heat and stir in half the cheese.

Drain the spaghetti and and toss with beaten egg. Spray a 9 to 10-inch pie pan with nonstick cooking spray and spread spaghetti along bottom and sides to form a bowl-shaped crust. Spoon in the meat mixture. Bake, covered with foil, 30 minutes at 350 degrees. Uncover, sprinkle with remaining cheese, bake 10 minutes more. Let sit a few minutes before slicing.

Serves 6.

Comments

Food, like literature, is about nourishing the spirit as well as the body. Worm pie is one of those rare and wondrous dishes which gladdens the child within us ("Wow! Two of my favorite things in the whole wide world, spaghetti *and* pie!") without destroying the interiors of our arteries.

You can use eggplant and zucchini in this pie, too. Fresh oregano would be a nice addition. If you don't eat meat, you can just leave it out.

⅋

Pot-Au-Feu

I learned to make this from my friends in Lyon the year I lived there and decided I really wanted to be a writer and not a chiropractor. I wrote every day and was happy as a clam, even though it drove my brains nuts to be speaking French but writing English all the time. It was scary, coming back to a recession and no job, but I'd made up my mind. A couple of months later, I sold my first novel.

Ingredients

2 tablespoons mild olive oil
3 cloves garlic, minced
3 to 4 pounds clod or chuck roast, well trimmed
½ cup red wine
water
1 teaspoon each thyme, rosemary, and basil (or marjoram)
2 bay leaves
3 leeks, halved, scrubbed and chopped into 2-inch sections
2 bunches baby turnips, scrubbed but left whole
6 carrots, peeled and cut in 2-inch chunks

Directions

In a large Dutch oven or other heavy lidded pan, heat the oil and sauté the garlic. Sear the meat on both sides.

Add wine and enough water to barely cover the meat. Put the herbs, except for bay leaves, in a tea strainer or cheesecloth bag. Add to water, along with bay leaves. Simmer 2 to 3 hours, or until meat is tender.

Add vegetables and simmer another hour, until everything smells incredible and the meat is falling apart. Add salt to taste and a little more wine just before serving with crusty bread. Don't eat the bay leaves.

Serves 6 to 8.

Dean Whitlock has been a professional science fiction writer since 1987, following the publication of his first story (which he reports just having expanded into his first novel). Since then he has written plays, video scrips, and even scripted three murder mystery weekends for a Vermont inn. He still has a "day job" producing user manuals, a quarterly newsletter, and marketing materials for a small software firm. He reports his interests as "Kites, canoes, camping, and caving."

Dean Whitlock

¶Ⅾ

Rabbit Saddle Madeira

This recipe did not inspire my story "Roadkill" (it was invented at least a decade before I wrote the story), but I remembered it and prepared it while working on the story. In an early version, Bun's carcass got found and used. The first version which editor Gardner Dozois saw left out dinner but kept in the hide. To his credit, he made me change even that.

Ingredients

    2 rabbit saddles (or 1 rabbit cut in pieces)
    flour
    paprika
    1 cup Madeira
    2 large garlic gloves, crushed
    6 pepper corns
    1 tablespoon celery seed (or to taste)
    water to cover
    6 small potatoes (new potatoes are best)
    4 small onions

Directions

    Dredge meat in flour and sprinkle very heavily with paprika; brown in Dutch oven. Add Madeira, garlic, pepper corns, celery seed, and enough water to cover. Simmer over low heat 20 minutes. Add potatoes and onions and cook till done, about 30 minutes. Add water as needed while cooking.

About cooking rabbit

    The rabbit saddle is the stretch of back between the ribs and hips; it's considered the best part of the rabbit by gourmets. I'm just as happy with the entire rabbit cut into pieces. Snowshoe hare is more richly flavored but harder to get (you have to know a hunter and be willing to eat—and perhaps skin—his kill). If even a domestic rabbit is too strong for your ethics, you can substitute chicken. After all, they're not nearly so cute and you can buy them anywhere.

⅋D

Pasta Sauce
with Clams and Vegetables

We spend at least a week each year on the shore, poking around in the tidal zones. In the winter, we eat seafood for the memories as much as the flavor. My story "Three Gifts" was going to have a lot more in it about gleaning food from the magic zone between the tide lines, but I got distracted by the theme. That leaves me with another story to write (and more seafood recipes to invent).

Ingredients

    1 medium onion
    ½ red or yellow bell pepper
    1 stick celery
    2 garlic cloves
    ¼ cup olive oil
    ½ stick butter
    1 tablespoon flour
    1 can small clams or chopped clams
    water
    2 tablespoons fresh chopped parsely
    black pepper to taste
    1 large tomato

Directions

Coarsely chop the onion, yellow pepper, and celery; finely chop the garlic. Heat the oil and butter together in a medium saucepan; sauté the onion and celery for 1 to 2 minutes, then add the garlic and yellow pepper. Sprinkle in the flour and cook 3 minutes over medium heat, stirring constantly. Add the juice from the can of clams, plus enough water to make 1 cup; raise heat and simmer 1 minute. Add the clams, parsely, and black pepper; cook for as long as it takes to cube the tomato. Reduce heat, add the tomato and cook very briefly (the sauce around the tomato pieces should pinken slightly). Remove from heat and serve immediately on pasta (if you let it sit, the tomato will overcook). Sprinkle with freshly grated parmesen cheese.

This is just as good, if not better, with mussels, particularly if you pluck them yourself from cold Maine waters. Variations include adding mushrooms or olives with the clams. You can thicken the sauce by adding 2 tablespoons of grated parmesan when you add the clams. You can thin the sauce or make it richer by adding bottled clam juice. For pasta, I prefer serving this with radiatorre or spirals, but any good noodle will do. Experiment! (But don't overcook it.)

Kate Wilhelm has long been one of the premiere writers of science fiction and mysteries. Among her best-known works are The Killer Thing, Welcome, Chaos, *and* Death Qualified: A Mystery of Chaos. *She is married to fellow writer Damon Knight and was also instrumental in setting up the Clarion writers workshops.*

Kate Wilhelm

⅋

Puerco Verde

Ingredients

1 cup cooked tomatillos
1 onion, chopped
1 or 2 cloves garlic
4 jalapeño chilis (whole for a hotter sauce, deseeded for a milder sauce)
juice of 1 lime
¼ cup peanuts (or 2 tablespoons chunky peanut butter)
1 teaspoon salt
½ teaspoon thyme
pepper to taste
3 to 4 pounds boneless pork in one piece

Directions

Blend cooked tomatillos, onion, garlic, jalapeño chilis, lime juice, peanuts, salt, thyme, and pepper to make a thick paste.

Pierce the meat all over with a fork. Rub the salsa into the meat, and place in refrigerator overnight in a casserole that can go from the oven to the burner later. Turn the meat several times in the marinade.

Next day, cover the meat and bake in the marinade for about 2 hours at 350 degrees, or until well done but not falling apart. Turn it several times during the baking so that a brown crust forms over it all. When the meat is done, place it on a platter, cover, and keep warm.

Defat the pan juices thoroughly. Add a cup of water and stir to loosen the bits of sauce stuck to the pan. Let this simmer gently.

Either chop finely, or blend coarsely:

½ cup cilantro
½ cup parsley

4 lettuce leaves (dark green, or use spinach)
a few sprigs of mint
zest from the lime (finely grate only the green part of the rind)

Raise the heat and stir the pan juice until it has thickened slightly, or turned syrupy; add the green mixture and stir for about a minute. Slice the meat and arrange the slices in an overlapping pattern, pour the green sauce over the slices. Garnish with slices of lime. Serve with rice. This is very lightly salted; you may want to add additional salt to the green mixture.

M.K. Wren *studied professional writing at the University of Oklahoma in the early 1960s, but didn't become series about writing until 1970. Her first project—a mystery entitled* Curiosity Didn't Kill the Cat—*appeared from Doubleday in 1973. She continues to write mysteries about her series character, Conan Joseph Flagg, while penning the occasional science fiction novels such as* A Gift Upon the Shore *and* The Phoenix Legacy. *Currently she lives in Oregon.*

M. K. Wren

🍴

The LoHi Option
(a. k. a. Egg Burrito)

This is a brunch item. I usually cook one at a time, but it probably wouldn't be difficult to make two. I'm not sure about more. The question with the LoHi Option is how healthily virtuous you want to be. You can make it low in evil cholesterol and calories or hedonistically high.

Ingredients

egg (or virtuous ersatz egg)
sliced or diced onion-red, white, yellow, or green (whatever)
medium-size flour tortilla
grated cheese (sinful aged cheddar or virtuous mozzarella)
lettuce, plain or fancy
sprouts (I prefer radish sprouts, but if you want to try them, you'll probably
    have to grow your own)
salsa

Directions

Use your favorite small skillet, preferably the old grungy iron one, on medium or medium-high heat. Melt a little butter in the skillet (or a little virtuous margarine or spray with totally virtuous Pam). Break the egg (if you opt for sin) into a bowl and stir furiously with a fork. Next, throw enough onion in the skillet to cover the bottom in a lacy pattern.

While the onion is cooking, zap the tortilla in the microwave for 20 seconds on high power. Butter the tortilla, if you feel hedonistic, or margarine it, or use it virtuously virgin.

Pour the stirred (or ersatz) egg over the onion, tipping the skillet to fill all the little holes in the lace. Then scatter the grated cheese on top. Immediately turn off the heat, put on a tight lid, and let the cheese melt.

Next, lay a few pieces of lettuce in the middle of the tortilla. Remember, you have to leave enough naked tortilla at the bottom and sides so you can fold the thing up.

Check the egg/onion/cheese stuff to see if the cheese is melted. If so, spread a wad of sprouts on half of it, then fold the other half over it. (And/or sprinkle on some fresh, chopped chives or parsley.) It's ready to apply to the tortilla now, but there'll probably be too much, so use your spatula to trim out a piece that will fit nicely atop the lettuce. Fold up the tortilla. You'll need a toothpick to hold it together.

Keep the salsa bottle handy as you eat the LoHi Option, and spoon on to taste.